Montgomery County Community College

50 Years of Thinking Big

Montgomery County Community College

50 Years of Thinking Big

by Alana Mauger, Diana VanDyke, and John Galluzzo

Copyright © 2014 by Montgomery County Community College

All rights reserved, including the right to reproduce this work in any form whatsoever without permission in writing from the publisher, except for brief passages in connection with a review. For information, please write:

THE
DONNING COMPANY
PUBLISHERS

The Donning Company Publishers
184 Business Park Drive, Suite 206
Virginia Beach, VA 23462

Steve Mull, *General Manager*
Barbara Buchanan, *Office Manager*
Heather L. Floyd, *Editor*
Stephanie Danko, *Graphic Designer*
Kathy Adams, *Imaging Artist*
Susan Adams, *Project Research Coordinator*
Nathan Stufflebean, *Marketing and Research Supervisor*
Katie Gardner, *Marketing Assistant*

Mary Miller, *Project Director*

Library of Congress Cataloging-in-Publication Data

Mauger, Alana.
    Montgomery County Community College : 50 years of thinking big / by Alana Mauger, Diana Van-Dyke, and John Galluzzo.
        pages cm
        ISBN 978-1-57864-932-7 (hardcover : alk. paper)
 1. Montgomery County Community College—History. I. VanDyke, Diana. II. Galluzzo, John. III. Title.
    LD6501.M644M48 2014
    378.154309748'12--dc23
                                                                2014040164

Printed in the United States of America at Walsworth Publishing Company

Contents

A Message from President Dr. Karen A. Stout 7

50 Years of Thinking Big: A Timeline 8

    The Community College Idea 9
    Montgomery County Community College's First President, Dr. LeRoy Brendlinger 12
    Conshohocken 13
    Montgomery County Community College Moves to Blue Bell 40
    Faculty Strikes 61
    Second President Dr. Edmund Watters III 63
    Dr. Edward Sweitzer Named Third President 64
    More Than a "Space to Create": The Arts at Montgomery County Community College 66
    The College Expands into Pottstown 72
    Dr. Karen A. Stout Named Fourth President 78
    Montco Radio: Streaming 24/7 Online 82
    Climate Leadership 89
    Achieving the Dream 93
    Mustangs Athletics Returns to Campus 94
    Veterans Find Support, Compassion, and Camaraderie at the College 100
    Virtual Campus 121
    The Culinary Arts Institute at Montgomery County Community College 122

MONTGOMERY COUNTY COMMUNITY COLLEGE'S MISSION

MONTGOMERY COUNTY COMMUNITY COLLEGE is a place where the future is created and desire and knowledge are combined to yield opportunity. The College reflects and responds to the needs and aspirations of those who live, work, and conduct business in Montgomery County and beyond. Grounded in a set of values that teaches us to encourage, listen, respect, and treat fairly those whom we serve, those with whom we work, and those who work with us in service, the College strives to ensure that all Montgomery County residents have access to the highest-quality and most affordable higher education possible. Most importantly, the College is dedicated to fostering the growth and success of everyone we serve.

    The College believes that learning is a lifelong activity requiring constant adaptation of programs, courses, and learning support services to reflect social, technology, and workforce changes and to ensure that all learners reach their unique goals.

    Believing in the right of everyone to have access to a quality education, workforce training, opportunities for personal and professional growth, and culture and recreation, the College translates the values of its community and reaches out to it, inviting involvement, offering learning, and fostering understanding.

A Message from President Dr. Karen A. Stout

Fifty years ago, Montgomery County Community College was founded on the bold belief that education has the power to transform lives and communities. The College's early visionaries laid the framework for what we are today—a community hub for education, innovation, workforce training, and cultural activity.

As we celebrate our fiftieth anniversary year, the College is ever mindful of its founders' intent to serve the community by providing the highest-quality, affordable education and the pathways and support for our students to attain success. We continually assess, revise, and update our programs and curricula to ensure that they are relevant for today's and tomorrow's careers. Through all of our programs, we strive to prepare students to be multi-faceted, creative thinkers who are ready to work in any capacity—including jobs and fields that may not yet exist, but will be on their horizons.

We know, too, from our decades of serving the community, that our classrooms are filled with all types of learners—from the traditional high school graduates to career changers to those who desire to gain new skills or enrich their lives with new opportunities. The College is here to serve all of their varied needs and to encourage them to think big, achieve their goals, and be resilient during times of change.

The College's fiftieth anniversary offers us an ideal opportunity to reflect on our accomplishments, thank the people who made those achievements possible, and look forward to thinking bigger for the next fifty years and beyond.

Sincerely,

Dr. Karen A. Stout
President

50 Years of Thinking Big

A TIMELINE

1964

- Montgomery County Community College is established on December 8, 1964.

1965

- Frederick Peters files a lawsuit claiming the Community College Act is unconstitutional and an injunction is filed prohibiting the Board of Trustees to meet or act. Supreme Court Judge E. Arnold Forrest rules in favor of Peters and declares the Act unconstitutional.

- An Advisory Committee (LeRoy Brendlinger, Wilmot Fleming, and Jules Pearlstine) submits Act 322 of 1965, which amends Section 6 of the Community College Act of 1963. The amendment is approved and plans for the College proceed.

THE COMMUNITY COLLEGE IDEA

PENNSYLVANIANS TRIED FOR decades to get a junior or community college system in place. Talk of such a system began publicly in the 1920s, and the first steps toward legislation took place in 1937. Bills designed to allow for the formation of two-year urban colleges run by first-class school districts reappeared annually into the 1950s, but none passed.

Members of the College's original Board of Trustees in January 1965: (seated, from left) Dwight Dundore, Charles Kahn, Jr., Alice I. Anderson, Gladys C. Pearlstine, Dr. Joseph R. Feldmeier, Dr. Stephen W. Roberts, and Arthur A. Alderfer; (standing, from left) Herman B. Blumenthal, Edward J. Carroll, Thomas P. McArthur, Jr., R. Luther Young, Rev. Leonard M. Jones, William H. Harned, William E. Strasburg, and William H. Yohn, Sr.

In 1948, the state legislature called for a thorough examination of community colleges elsewhere in the country. However, it wasn't until 1961 that Governor David Lawrence's Committee on Education pushed the issue to the forefront, calling for immediate action. In December of that year, he appointed what he called the Governor's Committee of 100 for Better Education, charging it with swaying public opinion to the point that a bill introduced to the state legislature calling for the creation of community colleges might finally have a fighting chance at passing.

Locally in Montgomery County, community leaders identified their interest in extending opportunities for higher education as early as 1950. As a result, by 1961, key interest groups and individuals were already engaged in discussions about a possible community college. The Citizens Council of Montgomery County was formed in 1961, followed by the Committee to Extend Educational Opportunities in 1962. The latter produced a position paper on the need for a community college, stressing the growing technical nature of work in the county, and the call for a more skilled workforce by local industrial employers.

In May 1963, the committee released the results of a survey taken during the past winter of 20,000 tenth-, eleventh-, and twelfth-graders regarding a potential community college for Montgomery County. Thirty-five percent of the students claimed they would be interested in attending a community college in Montgomery County if one existed; that number represented 60 percent of the students from the county planning to attend postsecondary schooling. The report also cited positive reactions by local businesses to the concept.

During this time, the Governor's Committee of 100 for Better Education had formed a team of lobbyists charged with bringing the community college question to the desk of every state politician possible. They fueled the conversation on a statewide basis and began to sway public opinion, resulting in the introduction of eighteen different bills between 1961 and 1963 alone. Finally, in 1963, House Bill 1066, calling for the formation of community colleges under the sponsorship of any local authority, made it to the floor for debate. The bill passed the House 194 to 8, and the Senate 54 to 0. Governor William Scranton signed Act 484 of 1963 into law on August 24, entitling it "The Community College Act."

In 1964, the Montgomery County commissioners appointed a Community College Advisory Committee to investigate next steps, including formally applying to the State Board of Education and selecting a location for the school. Realizing that public opinion was crucial, a series of town hall meetings followed an extensive letter-writing campaign, spearheaded by Dr. LeRoy Brendlinger, who would become the College's first

Dr. LeRoy Brendlinger was instrumental in building momentum for the community college in his role as assistant superintendent for Montgomery County schools long before he was named the College's founding president in 1964.

Dedication of Montgomery County Community College on October 18, 1966: (from left) Daniel T. Costello, county commissioner; A. Russell Parkhouse, president, county commissioners; William W. Scranton, governor of Pennsylvania; William W. Vogel, county commissioner; Dr. LeRoy Brendlinger, College president; and Wilmot E. Fleming, state senator.

Montgomery County Commissioner A. Russell Parkhouse helps to inaugurate founding president Dr. LeRoy Brendlinger in 1966.

president. On June 1, 1964, the commissioners passed a resolution establishing Montgomery County Community College, and an appointed fifteen-member Board of Trustees met for the first time on January 5, 1965.

A lawsuit, filed by former county commissioner Frederick Peters on January 18, 1965, claiming the Community College Act was unconstitutional, delayed the College's opening for one year. The rewritten Act was approved on October 26, 1965, allowing the trustees to continue their work. On April 12, 1966, they selected the former Conshohocken High School as a temporary location for the school. Montgomery County Community College finally opened its doors on October 3, 1966.

The vacant Conshohocken High School building before the College moved in.

1966

- Dr. LeRoy Brendlinger is appointed the College's first president, serving in that capacity until his retirement in 1981.

MONTGOMERY COUNTY COMMUNITY COLLEGE'S FIRST PRESIDENT, DR. LEROY BRENDLINGER

As an educator and lifelong Montgomery County resident, Dr. LeRoy Brendlinger (1918–2011) was an early advocate for community colleges. In the early 1960s, he led a citizen steering committee to develop the plans that eventually established Montgomery County Community College.

Appointed as the first president in 1966, he guided the College from before its founding in 1964 until his retirement in 1981. Dr. Brendlinger firmly believed education has the power to transform lives and communities. That belief—coupled with his passion, vision, and leadership—has enabled the College to thrive for more than fifty years and to serve more than 400,000 students.

Before serving as the College's president, Dr. Brendlinger was the assistant superintendent of county schools in Montgomery County. He also held positions as teacher and principal at several area schools, and he spent four years in the U.S. Army during World War II. He graduated from West Chester University with a bachelor's degree in education and earned a master's degree in education from the University of Pennsylvania and an Ed.D. from Temple University.

Even after his retirement in 1981, Dr. Brendlinger remained active in the life of the College. He maintained an office in the Central Campus library, which was re-named The Brendlinger Library in 2004 in his honor.

- The College begins serving the community at the former Conshohocken High School building, located at 7th and Fayette streets, Conshohocken. The doors opened on October 3, 1966, with seventeen faculty and 428 students. The Opening Day dedication is held on October 18, 1966.

CONSHOHOCKEN

Delayed by the lawsuit and scheduled to open in October 1966, the Board of Trustees did not have time to consider permanent sites and new construction by the time it began its formal work in March 1966. The trustees' initial choice—the site that is now Temple University's Ambler Campus—was no longer available. Fortunately, the former Conshohocken High School building was available after a recent merger with a neighboring school district.

Publically thought to be condemned, a call to the state education commission proved this was not the case. However, as an aging facility, the Conshohocken campus presented all of the problems associated with older buildings: inadequate space for classrooms and offices, inconsistent heating and lack of air conditioning, lights that dimmed when the streetlights turned on, snow and rain penetrating closed windows and walls, the windows themselves falling in or out, noise from trucks gearing down for the Fayette Street hill, plaster detaching from the ceiling, and a severe lack of parking.

By the time the College was ready to move into its permanent home on the 186-acre farm in Blue Bell, classrooms and offices were spaced out miles apart in Conhohocken as more space was rented to accommodate the increasing student population. Classes were held in any space available, including above Flocco's Shoe Store and in a former funeral home. Library Hall was a former Presbyterian church; the Heywood Building, next to the main building, housed administrative offices; the Student Center and Student Affairs offices were located in renovated houses; and the Admissions and Business offices were in a former office building. During registration, students would line up on the street waiting to register for classes.

In 1966–1967, full-time equivalent enrollment averaged 500 students per semester. That figure doubled by 1967–1968 and tripled by 1968–1969. The College opened with seventeen full-time teaching faculty, two non-teaching faculty (a librarian and a counselor), three administrators (the president, the dean of academic affairs, and the director of business affairs), and ten support staff (secretaries and maintenance). By the fall of 1967, faculty positions increased to sixty-nine, and the College was offering thirteen areas of study, the majority of which were focused on transfer.

The College's first campus was at the corner of 7th and Fayette streets in Conshohocken. It quickly expanded throughout the town.

Lines of students wait outside the Admissions and Business offices.

Lines of students wait to register for classes.

Library Hall was a former Presbyterian Church.

Left: A typical classroom in the former Conshohocken High School.

Middle: Lack of parking in town led to many parking tickets in the early days of the College.

Right: Parking was a major issue for the College's early students.

Below: Students and faculty recall their time in converted classrooms above Flocco's Shoe Store.

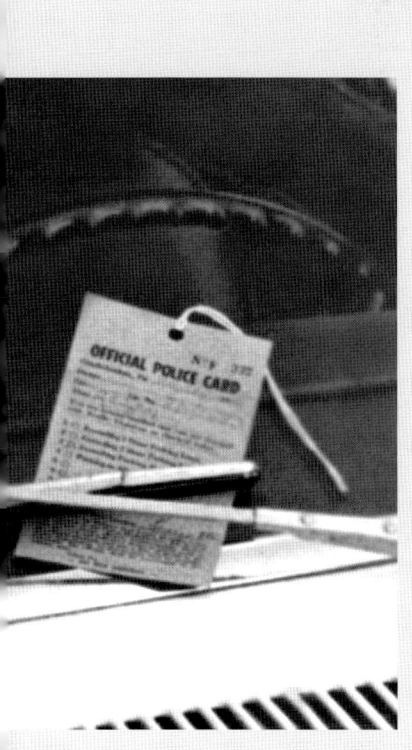

THIS PAGE AND OPPOSITE: *Students gather between classes at the College's original campus in Conshohocken.*

1967

- Students form the Student Government Assemblymen (later called the Student Government Association). Other clubs—including the social organization Triad, *The Montgazette* student newspaper, and a business club—soon follow.

First-ever staff of the College's student newspaper, The Montgazette: *(from left) Gidget Gayton, Carol Gayton, Karen Mignatti, James Heslin, John Ehinger, Joseph Gondek, Allen Burman, and Margaret Hoffmeri.*

Members of the Student Government Assemblymen in 1967–1968: (from left) Pat Geschke, Lorraine Di Giovanni, Diane King, Joe Sondek, Jim Yost, Dave Bucher, Jay Slepner, Linda Kramer, Ron Beaumont, Ann Gray, Lois Chase, and Regina Salmon.

Triad had the most members of any organization on campus in 1967–1968. The club was responsible for planning social and cultural activities for the College's students. Pictured are the Triad officers from 1968: (from left) Frankie Hoff, Sandra White, John Moscway, George Charters, and Diana King.

A member of the Student Government Association in 1969, John Kolb (seated) went on to serve as the first-ever president of the College's Alumni Association and later as a member of the College's Board of Trustees. He was inducted into the College's Alumni Hall of Fame in 2009.

MONTGOMERY COUNTY COMMUNITY COLLEGE 50 YEARS OF THINKING BIG | 21

THIS PAGE AND OPPOSITE: A look at some of the classroom and administrative buildings that comprised the College's Conshohocken campus.

ABOVE AND RIGHT: *Images from the College's days in Conshohocken.*

24 | MONTGOMERY COUNTY COMMUNITY COLLEGE 50 YEARS OF THINKING BIG

Students work in the College's original library, which was housed in a former church.

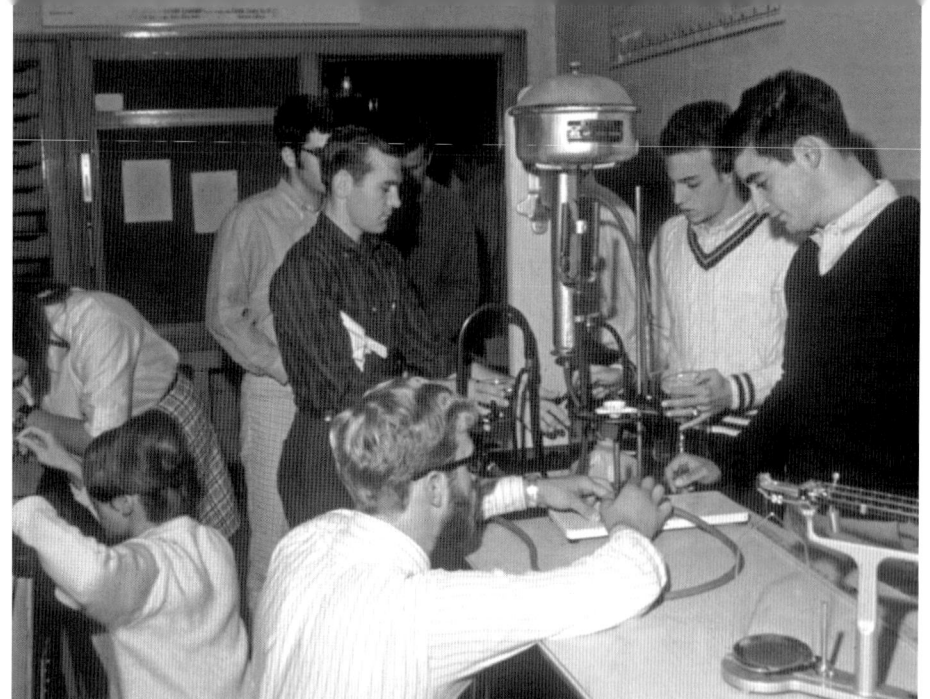

26 | MONTGOMERY COUNTY COMMUNITY COLLEGE 50 YEARS OF THINKING BIG

THIS PAGE AND OPPOSITE:
Images from the College's days in Conshohocken.

MONTGOMERY COUNTY COMMUNITY COLLEGE 50 YEARS OF THINKING BIG | 27

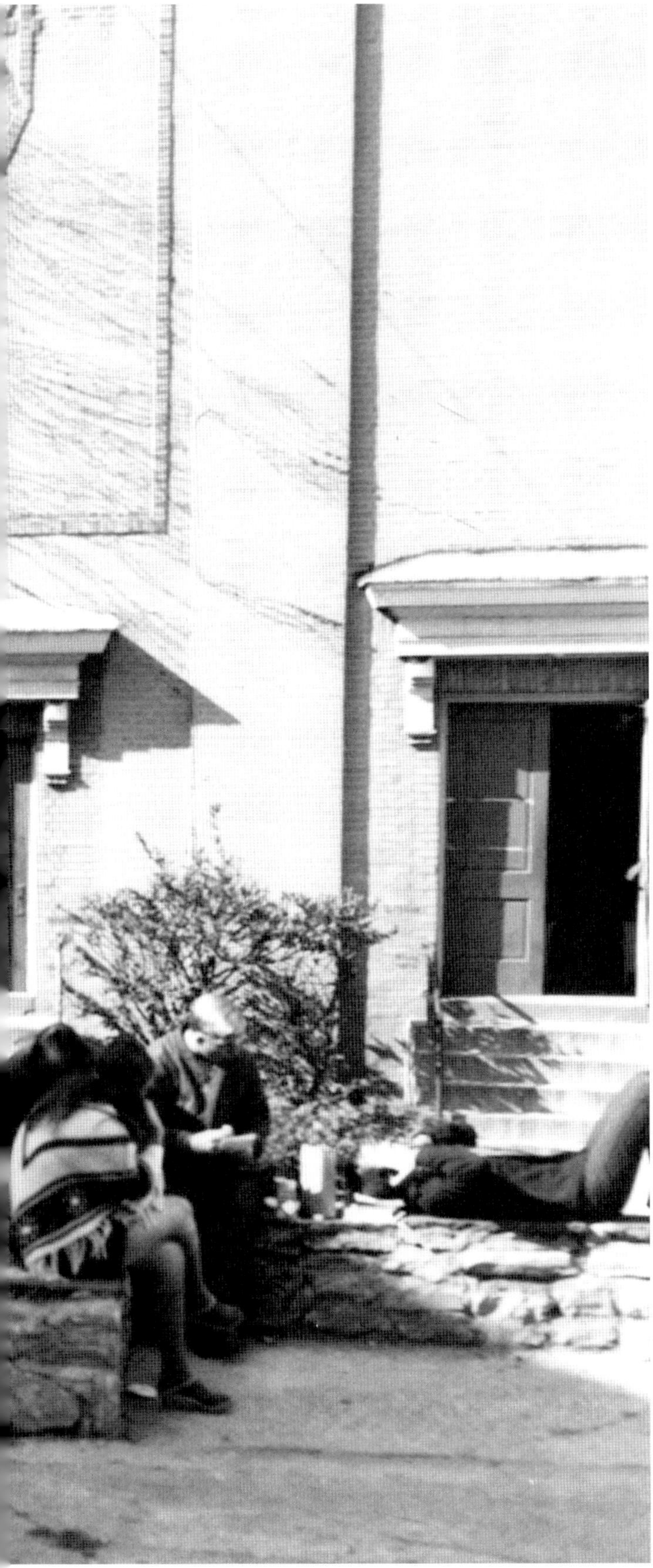

FAYETTE ST.
E. SEVENTH AVE.

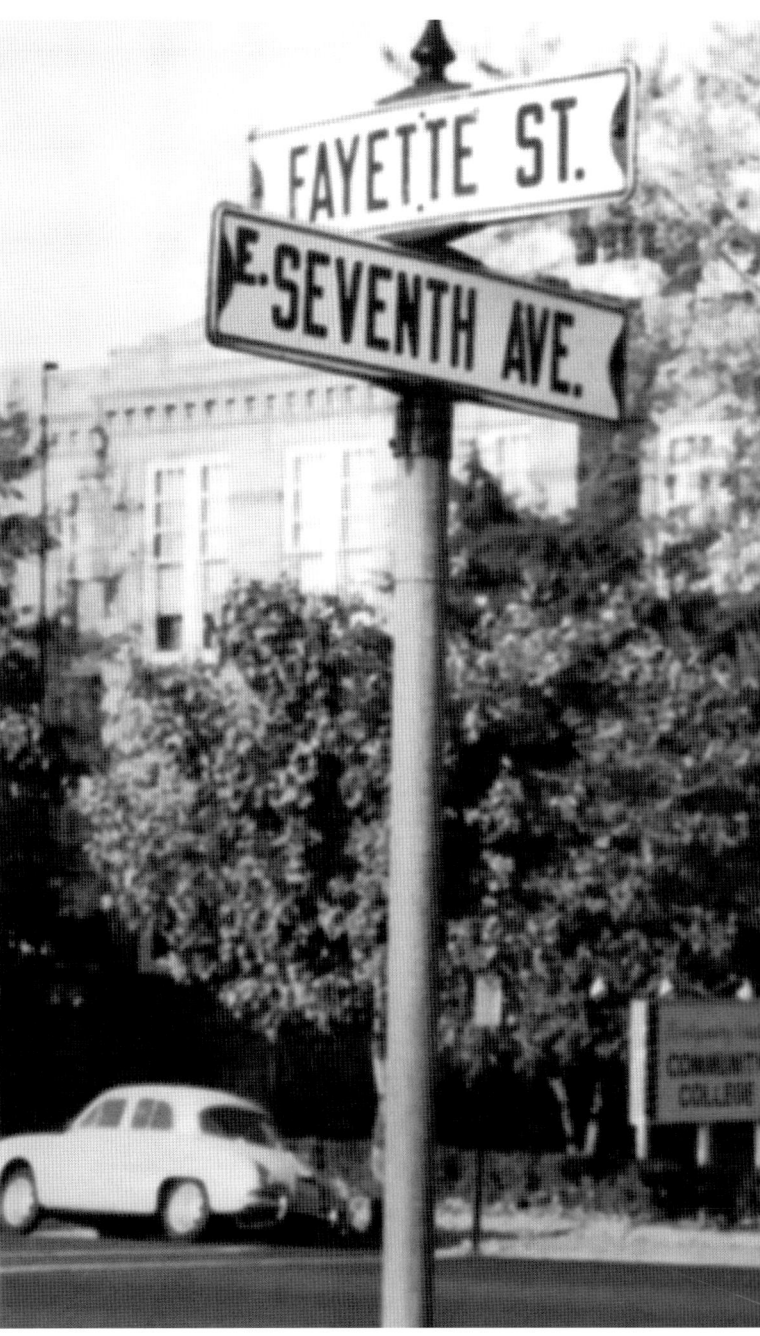

President Dr. LeRoy Brendlinger crowns the first "Miss Montco" queen Kathleen King in 1967.

1967 (cont.)

- December 8 is declared Founders' Day.

The College held its first Founders' Day celebration on December 8, 1967. Pictured here, Dr. Brendlinger (right) and State Representative Sieber Panacoast cut a Founders' Day cake in 1977 after the College's move to Blue Bell.

1968

- The College's first class graduates.

32 | MONTGOMERY COUNTY COMMUNITY COLLEGE 50 YEARS OF THINKING BIG

THIS PAGE AND OPPOSITE: *Images from the College's early commencement ceremonies between 1968 and 1971 in Conshohocken.*

1968 (cont.)

- The College purchases the Thayer Estate in Blue Bell for $700,000 for its new campus.

1969

- The first Middle States Commission on Higher Education evaluation visit is conducted (1969), and full accreditation is offered on April 27, 1970.

- Sports teams enter intercollegiate play as part of the Eastern Pennsylvania Community College Athletic Conference (EPCCAC). Initial teams include men's soccer, wrestling, basketball, and golf.

- The Faculty Senate is formed at the urging of Middle States to encourage greater faculty involvement in College-wide decision-making.

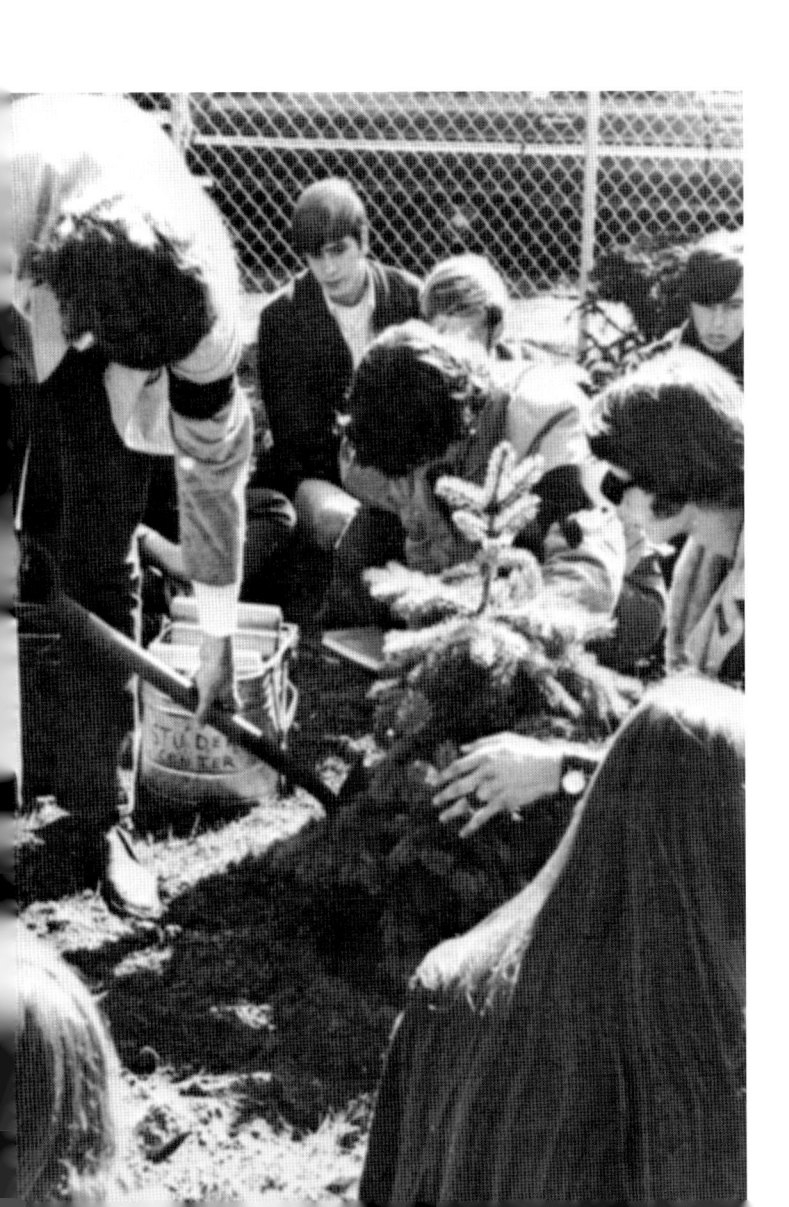

The men's basketball team, 1968–1969.

- Students plant "The Peace Tree" to honor those who were injured or killed in Vietnam. The tree is later moved to Blue Bell. After being transplanted several times, the tree was replaced and is now marked with a plaque outside of the current Fine Arts Center at the Central Campus.

1970

❧ A groundbreaking ceremony is held for the future Central Campus in Blue Bell on February 16, 1970.

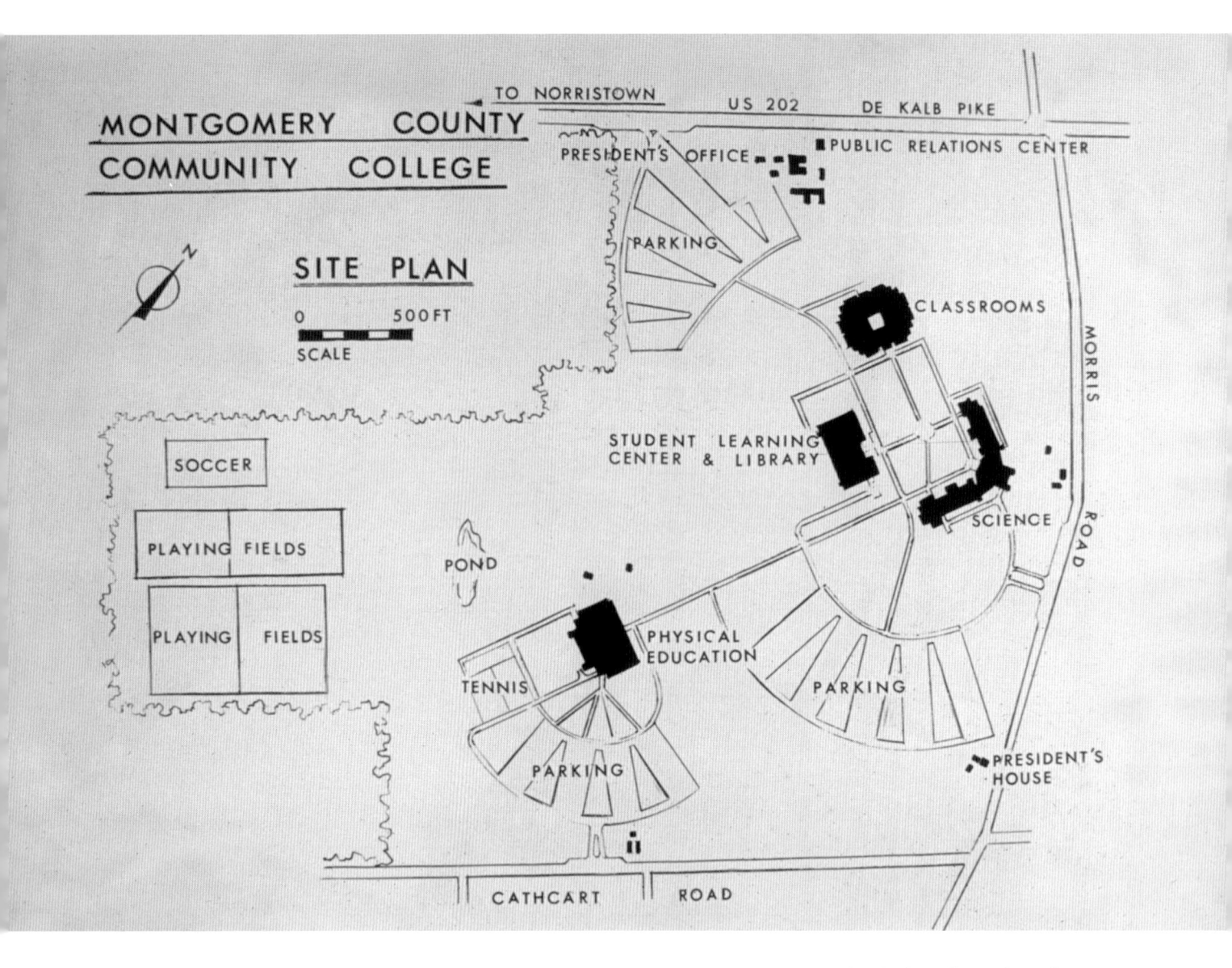

A site plan for the College's Blue Bell campus.

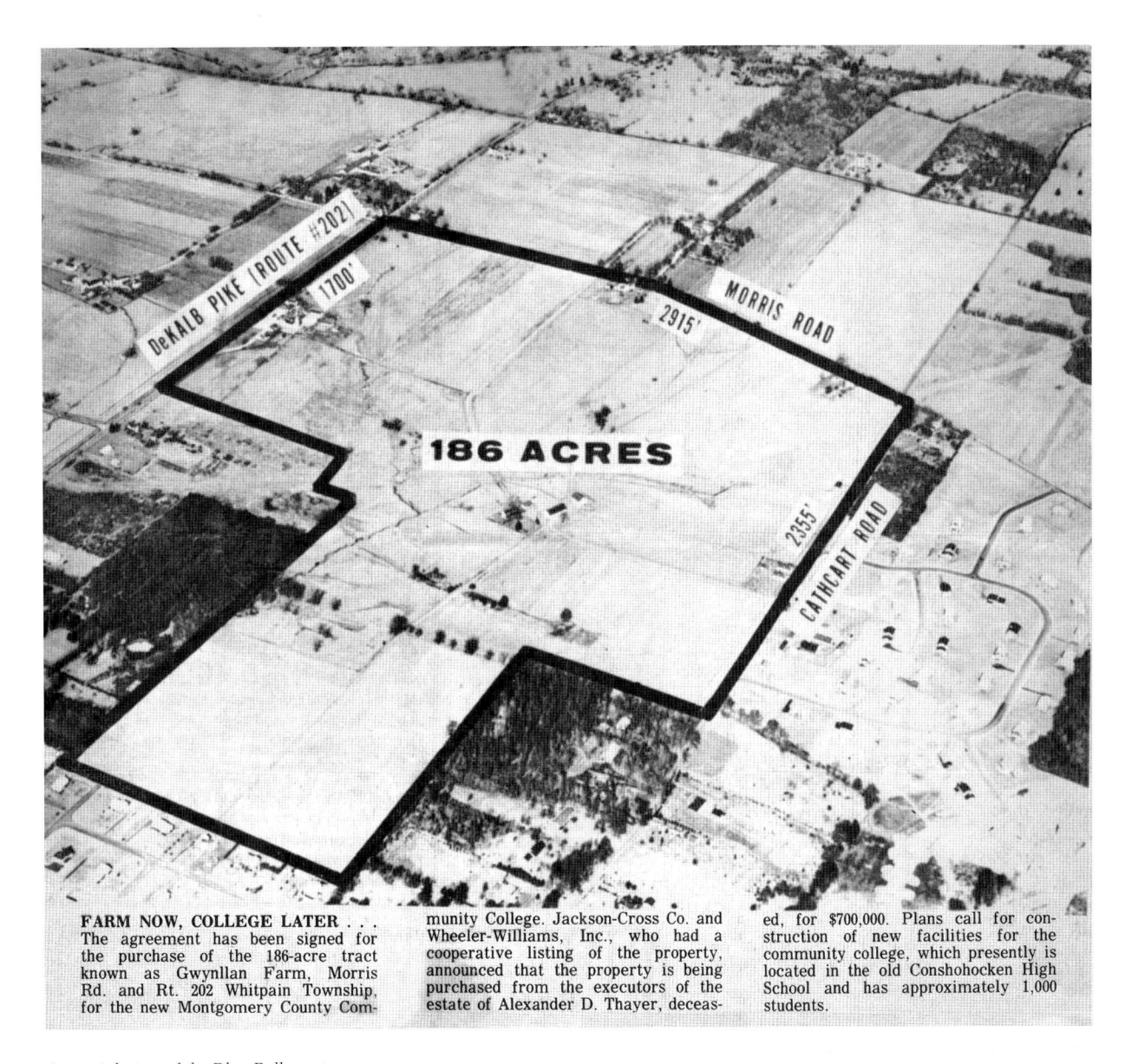

FARM NOW, COLLEGE LATER . . . The agreement has been signed for the purchase of the 186-acre tract known as Gwynllan Farm, Morris Rd. and Rt. 202 Whitpain Township, for the new Montgomery County Community College. Jackson-Cross Co. and Wheeler-Williams, Inc., who had a cooperative listing of the property, announced that the property is being purchased from the executors of the estate of Alexander D. Thayer, deceased, for $700,000. Plans call for construction of new facilities for the community college, which presently is located in the old Conshohocken High School and has approximately 1,000 students.

An aerial view of the Blue Bell campus from a newspaper clip circa 1970.

RIGHT: *Officials break ground for the College's Blue Bell campus in 1970.*

BELOW: *An aerial view of the Blue Bell campus shortly after opening.*

38 | MONTGOMERY COUNTY COMMUNITY COLLEGE 50 YEARS OF THINKING BIG

1970 (cont.)

- The Nursing program is introduced in 1970.

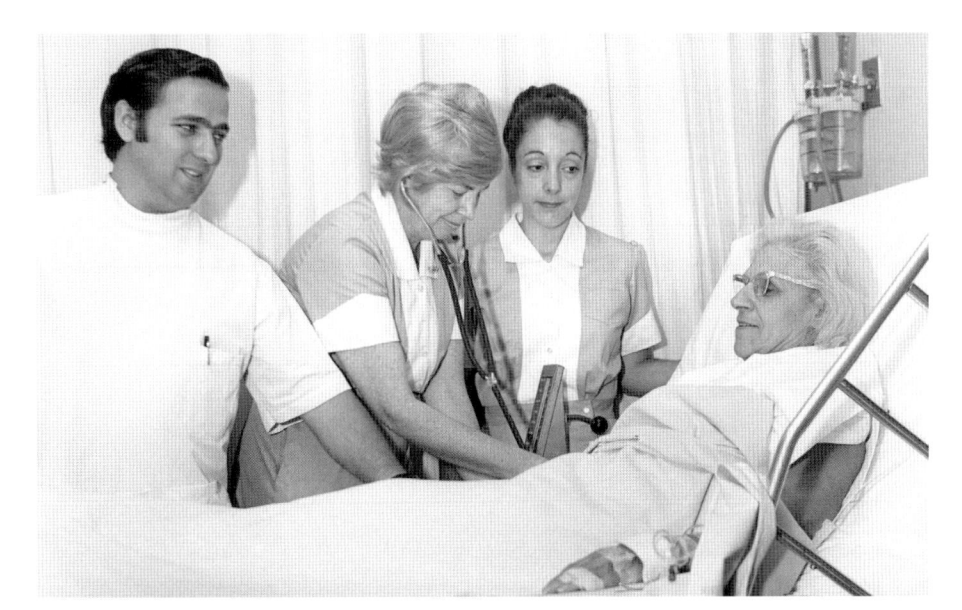

Early Nursing program students.

Students graduate from the College's Nursing program during a ceremony in Conshohocken.

1972

✣ The Central Campus opens, and by the fall of 1972, nearly 4,000 full- and part-time students are enrolled.

MONTGOMERY COUNTY COMMUNITY COLLEGE MOVES TO BLUE BELL

THE CONSHOHOCKEN CAMPUS with its eclectic mixture of buildings and classrooms was not intended to be a permanent home for the College, and the site subcommittee started searching for a new location in 1966. The subcommittee, led by Harry N. Gasser, assistant county superintendent of schools, looked for a location in the center of the county and eventually placed a bid on the 186-acre Thayer property that had once been a part of Gwynllan Farm.

Construction of the new campus began following the groundbreaking ceremony on February 16, 1970. The new campus would have four major buildings—a library/student center, classroom building, science center, and gymnasium—as well as fields for sports and parking lots.

Construction started on schedule but unfortunately was hampered by a laborers' strike. Additionally, the contractors ran into problems when building the physical education building after discovering that a spring existed at the building site.

Despite the difficulties, construction continued and careful consideration was given to the environmental attributes of the property. As a result of the concerns of Biology faculty member Richard Andren, grasslands and a pond were preserved to provide spaces for wildlife.

Construction concluded in the fall of 1971, and the new campus opened in 1972 for the spring semester. Dedication ceremonies were held on March 26, 1972, when the final cornerstone was placed in College Hall.

Before leaving Conshohocken, the College, along with the Junior Chamber of Commerce, prepared a farewell event. They declared November 5 as "Conshohocken Appreciation Day," and President Dr. Brendlinger presented a plaque to Mayor DiJiosia.

Building the College's permanent home in Blue Bell.

President Dr. LeRoy Brendlinger and Commissioner A. Russell Parkhouse placed a time capsule in the cornerstone of Founders Hall when the Blue Bell campus opened.

Construction on College Hall.

Painting in the Art Barn, a preserved building from the Thayer Estate.

The former Mechanical Engineering lab in the Science Center.

The College Hall information desk in the early years of the College's Blue Bell campus.

ABOVE: *Students walk to class at the College's Blue Bell campus.*

RIGHT: *Richard Andren works with students in one of the College's Biology laboratories.*

44 | MONTGOMERY COUNTY COMMUNITY COLLEGE 50 YEARS OF THINKING BIG

LEFT: Ray Leary teaches students Chemistry fundamentals.

BELOW: Larry Elias works with a student in an early Computer Science course.

Hospitality Management students practice their skills at the Blue Bell campus.

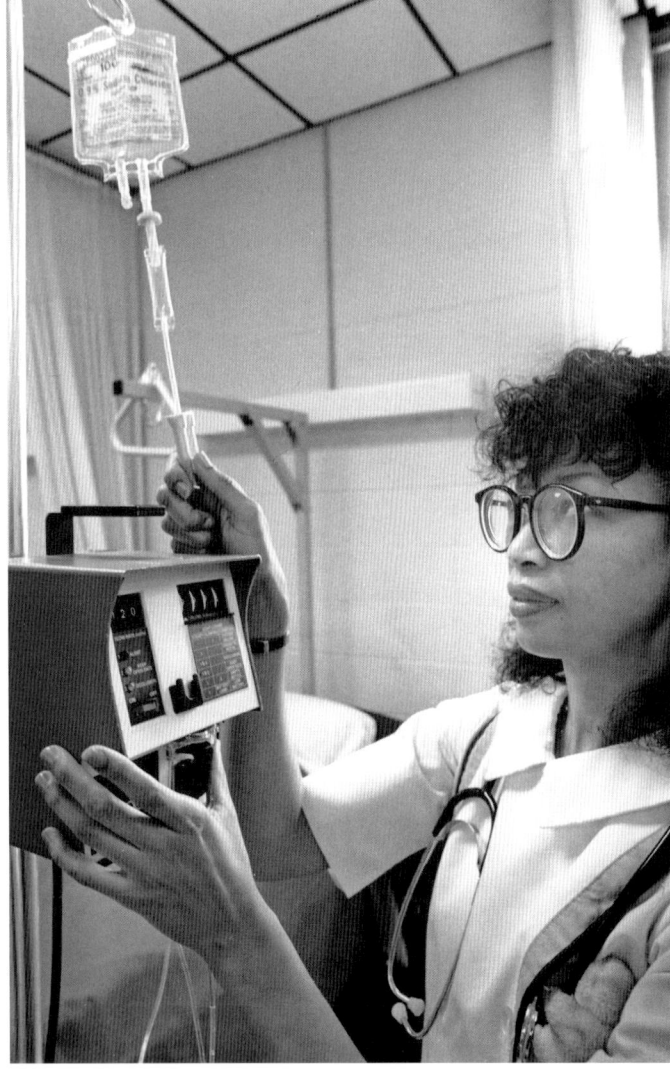

A Nursing student learns how to monitor an IV in the College's Nursing lab.

Men's basketball was among the Mustangs' earliest sports teams.

RIGHT: James Randolph teaches archery to Physical Education students at the College's Blue Bell campus.

BELOW: Wrestling was a popular sport in the College's early years in Blue Bell.

Field hockey was an early popular women's sport at the College.

English Professor Zygunt Wardzinski teaches class in the Founders Hall courtyard in Blue Bell.

LEFT AND BELOW: *Students on campus between classes.*

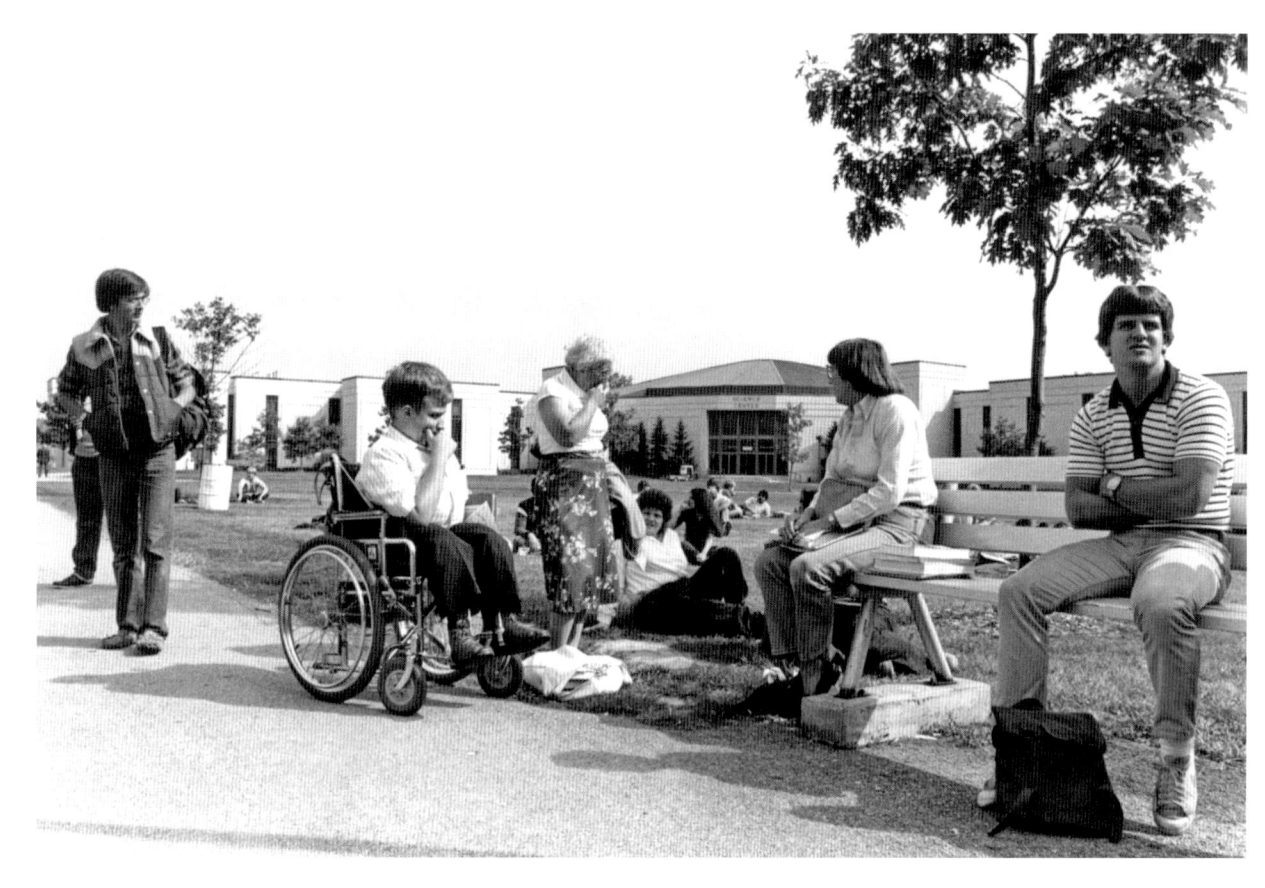

ABOVE AND LEFT: *Students on campus between classes.*

English Professor Bonnie Finkelstein teaches class in the Founders Hall courtyard in Blue Bell.

ABOVE: *Alex Leinbach instructs students in media technologies.*

RIGHT: *A students observes specimens in one of the College's Biology laboratories.*

Above and left: Graduation images from an early ceremony at the College's Blue Bell campus.

MONTGOMERY COUNTY COMMUNITY COLLEGE 50 YEARS OF THINKING BIG | 55

William Toplis teaches biology to students at the Blue Bell campus.

Biology students learn to use microscopes.

56 | MONTGOMERY COUNTY COMMUNITY COLLEGE 50 YEARS OF THINKING BIG

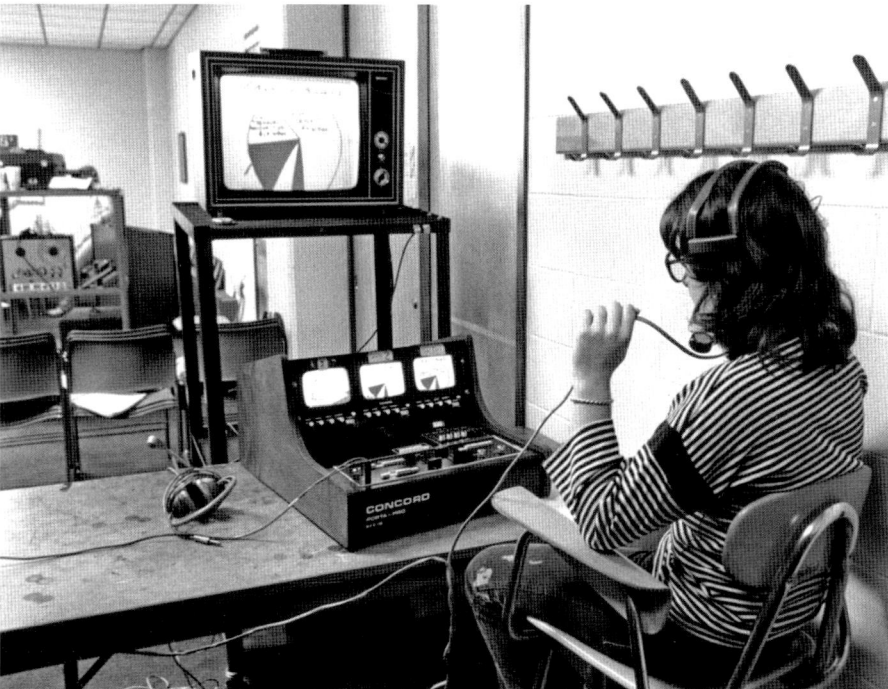

ABOVE AND LEFT: *Students learn early media technologies circa 1977 in Blue Bell.*

1972 (cont.)

- The men's basketball team wins the EPCCAC championship.

1973

- The Dental Hygiene program is introduced in the fall of 1973.

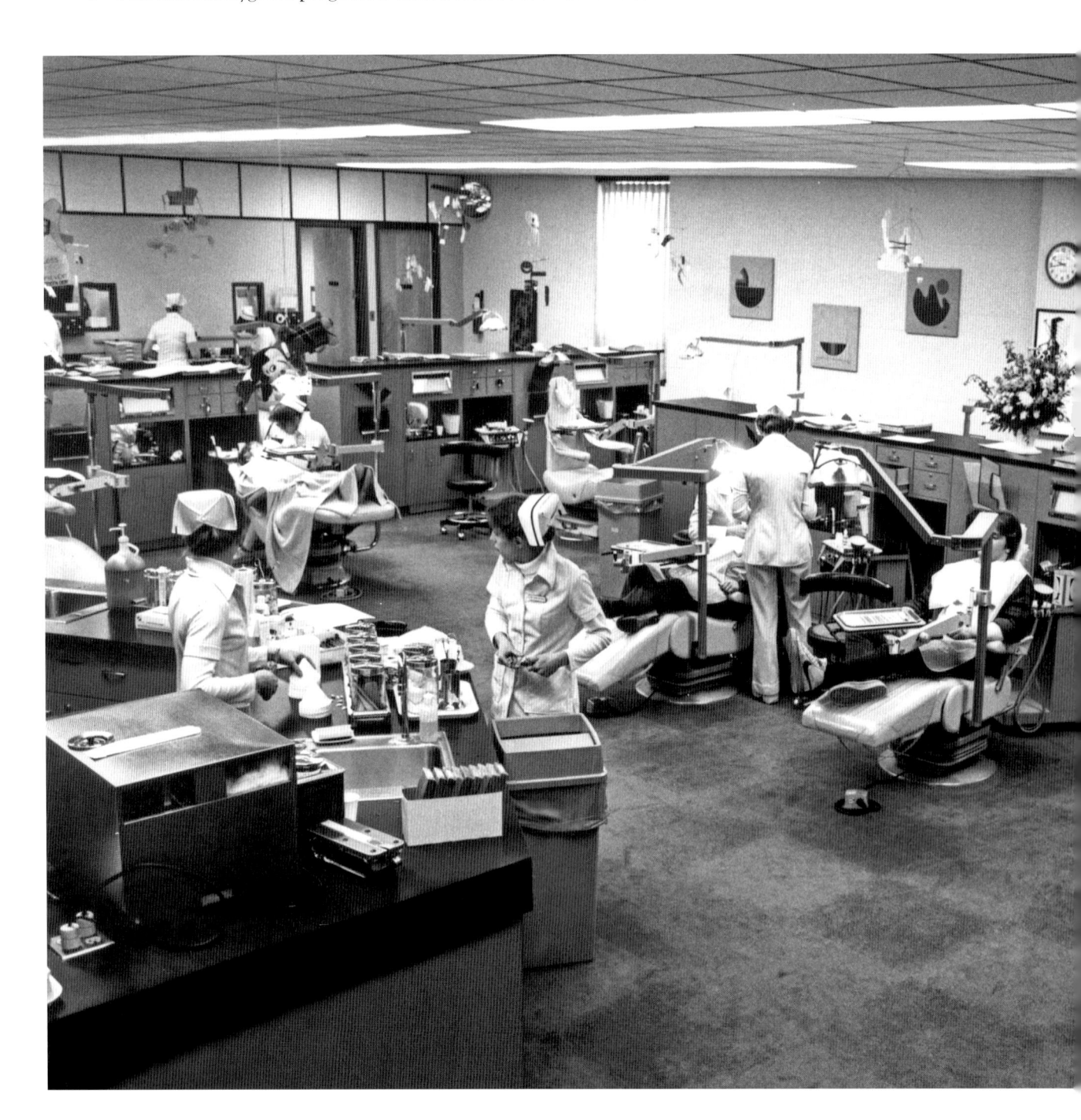

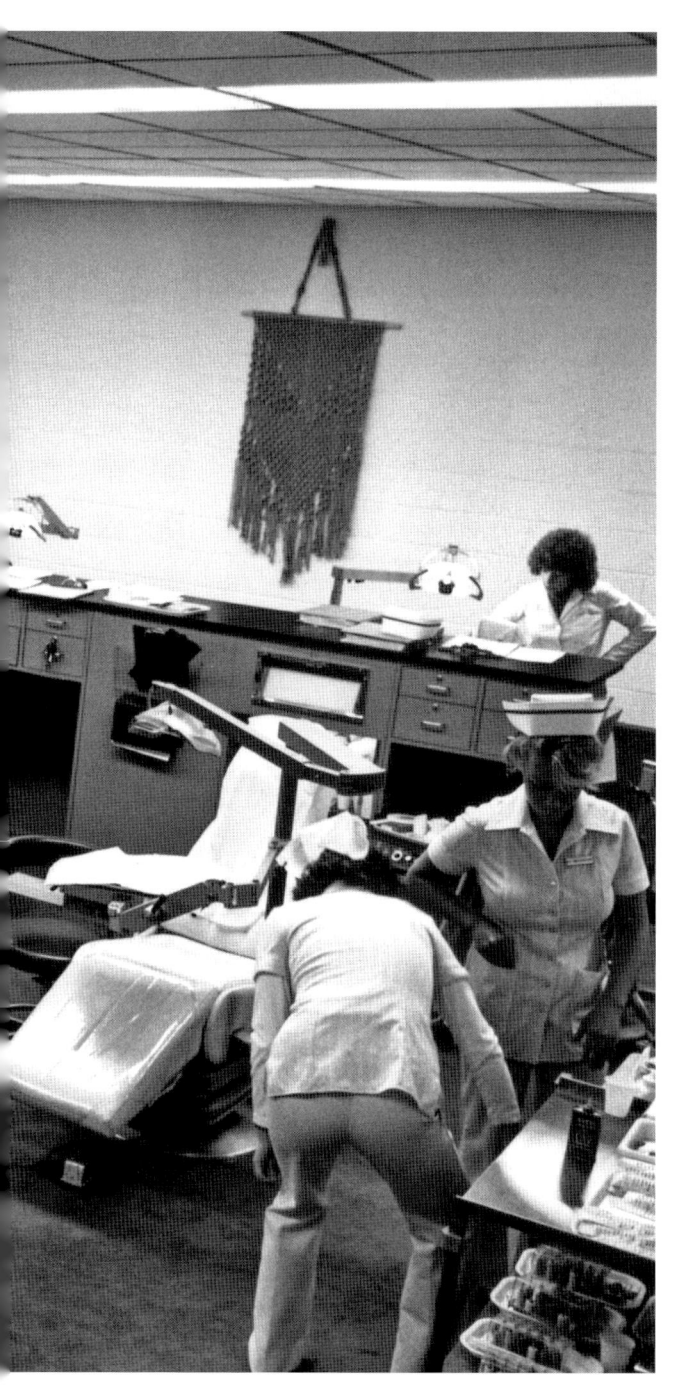

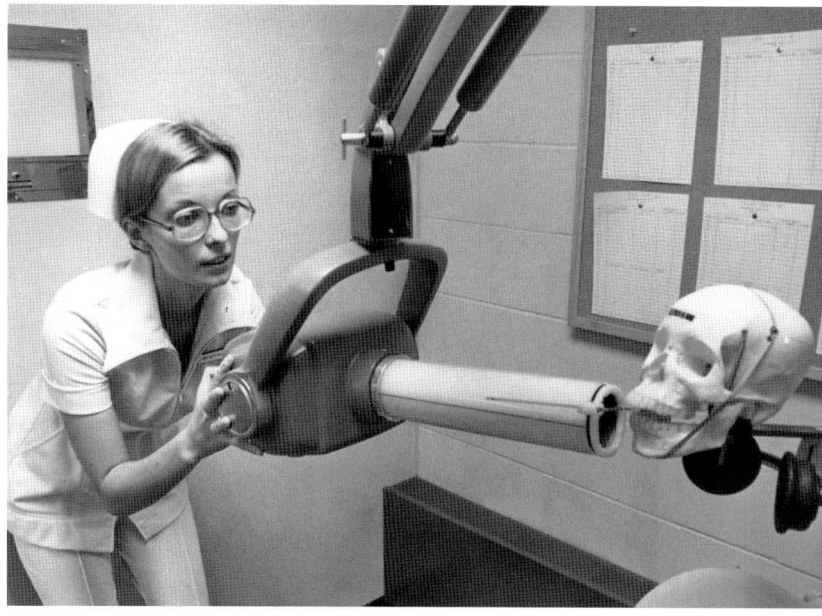

An early Dental Hygiene student practices taking an X-ray in the Dental Hygiene laboratory at the Central Campus.

Students learn in the brand-new Dental Hygiene laboratory at the College's Central Campus in 1973.

MONTGOMERY COUNTY COMMUNITY COLLEGE 50 YEARS OF THINKING BIG | 59

1974

- The soccer team wins its third straight EPCCAC crown.

The 1973 Mustangs soccer team.

1975

- The American Dental Association's Commission on Accreditation accredits the College's Dental Hygiene program.
- The soccer team wins its fourth EPCCAC crown.

1977

- The Medical Laboratory Technician program is introduced in the fall of 1977.

1979

- Faculty vote to unionize and join the American Association of University Professors (AAUP).

1980

- A "Snow Day" strike takes place on March 31–April 1, 1980, during which the College closes for two days so that contract negotiations could continue.

FACULTY STRIKES

In his book, *Ah Montco, What a Place!*, Charles E. Reilly writes that "from 1977 through 1983, Montgomery County Community College went through its 'teens,' [and] as is often the case, the teenage years were turbulent."

The College's faculty voted to unionize in 1979, becoming members of the American Association of University Professors (AAUP) and dissolving the Faculty Senate. During a thirty-month period that followed, the College coped with the impact of three faculty strikes.

While not a conventional strike, the College was closed on March 31–April 1, 1980, for what is now called the "Snow Day" strike. Having had a mild winter, the administration used two snow days built into the academic calendar so that contract negotiations could continue. The College reopened on April 2.

The College's first conventional strike began on September 3, 1981, and was resolved on September 28. Then, thirteen months later, the third strike—a mid-semester walk out—began on October 12, 1982, and was settled on November 9.

The students—most of whom grew up surrounded by Vietnam War protests—got involved. They staged rallies on campus, wrote letters to Board members, and covered every development in *The Montgazette*. Prior to the 1982 strike, several student clubs organized a Student Solidarity Day on September 16 to demand action in the faculty negotiations.

ABOVE: *A view of College Hall from the Science Center's second floor at the Blue Bell campus.*

RIGHT: *Students study in the College Hall Library.*

62 | MONTGOMERY COUNTY COMMUNITY COLLEGE 50 YEARS OF THINKING BIG

1980 (cont.)

- The women's basketball team wins its first-ever Pennsylvania Women's Basketball Championship.

1981

- Dr. Edmund Watters III becomes the College's second president, serving from 1981 to 1987.

SECOND PRESIDENT DR. EDMUND WATTERS III

Dr. Edmund Watters III served as the College's second president from 1981 to 1987. Prior to his work in education, he served as an officer in the United States Army in Germany, during the Cold War days of the early 1960s. In 1966, he led a team of students to Botswana to help construct that country's first secondary school science laboratory. He completed his graduate and postgraduate studies at Lehigh University, earning his doctorate in education with a focus on community college administration. Before coming to the College in 1980 as dean of academic affairs, Watters served as assistant director of admissions at Lehigh, as a faculty member at both Wilkes College and Bucks County Community College, and from 1974 to 1981 as the chief academic officer at Williamsport Area Community College.

- A faculty strike begins on September 3, 1981, and is settled on September 28.

1982

- Student clubs organize a Student Solidarity Day on September 16 to demand action in faculty negotiations.

- A faculty strike begins on October 12, 1982, and is settled on November 9, 1982.

- The Science Center goes under major renovations.

1983

- The Foundation, the charitable arm of the College, is established.

1988

- Dr. Edward Sweitzer becomes the third president. He serves the College until his death in 2000.

DR. EDWARD SWEITZER NAMED THIRD PRESIDENT

Dr. Edward M. Sweitzer was selected by the College's Board of Trustees as the College's third president on June 21, 1988, serving until his death on May 8, 2000. Founding trustee and former board chairman Dwight Dundore described Sweitzer as leading "Montgomery County Community College through a period of major growth and change with a mixture of keen administrative and leadership skills, a wry sense of humor and a fit for putting students, faculty and staff alike at ease."

Prior to entering the arena of education administration, Dr. Sweitzer was a botanist, holding master's and doctorate degrees in botany from the University of Maryland. He held academic and administrative positions at Northern Virginia Community College before coming to the College as the dean of academic affairs in 1983. His work included a dissertation on "Comparative Anatomy and Taxonomy of *Ulmaceae*."

Under Dr. Sweitzer's leadership, the College introduced almost a dozen new academic programs, underwent seamless Middle States reaccreditation, expanded to Pottstown with the construction of the West Campus, introduced distance learning, formed transfer agreements with seven four-year colleges and universities in the region, expanded Foundation endowments to nearly $3 million, introduced the Lively Arts Series, significantly increased the number of women and minority employees, and saw enrollment grow from 7,000 to 9,000 students.

Upon his passing, the Montgomery County Community College Foundation created a memorial fund in honor of Dr. Sweitzer with the notion of making real one of his longtime dreams—the construction of a memorial clock tower in the quadrangle at the Central Campus. The Sweitzer Memorial Bell Tower was dedicated in 2003.

Dr. Edward M. Sweitzer

The Sweitzer Memorial Bell Tower at the College's Central Campus in Blue Bell.

1988 (cont.)

- The Lively Arts Series is introduced, and the Writers Conference is held for first time.

MORE THAN A "SPACE TO CREATE": THE ARTS AT MONTGOMERY COUNTY COMMUNITY COLLEGE

Montgomery County Community College has valued and supported the arts as part of its mission since its founding. Beyond providing a "space to create" for students, the College has become a cultural destination in offering a global perspective to the community by presenting artists and performances from a multitude of cultures.

In 1988, under the leadership of President Edward Sweitzer, the College started what is now known as the Lively Arts Series. The program offers main-stage events from September through May including music, dance, and speakers, as well as student theatre, music, and dance performances. Additionally, the College hosts fifteen or more art exhibitions at its two Fine Arts galleries in Blue Bell and Pottstown featuring local and nationally known artists.

Student artwork on display via clothesline in Conshohocken.

Dance classes were taught at the College long before it became a major in 2009.

Since its inception, the Lively Arts Series has received ongoing funding support from the Pennsylvania Council on the Arts, National Endowment for the Arts, Pennsylvania Humanities Council, Five County Arts Funds, Mid-Atlantic Arts Foundation, Pennsylvania Performing Arts on Tour, Philadelphia Music Project, Dance Advance Programs of the Pew Center for Arts and Heritage, Chamber Music America, the National Dance Project, and the William Penn Foundation.

Members of the College's Chorus in 1973.

Through the support of these partners, the College hosted some of the country's most iconic authors, including Alex Haley, Norman Mailer, Joyce Carol Oates, Frank McCourt, and John Updike, as well as jazz luminaries, such as Ahmad Jamal, McCoy Tyner, Ron Carter, Mose Allison, and Abbey Lincoln. For dance performances, the Pittsburgh Ballet, Paul Taylor, Philanco, and the Dance Theatre of Harlem, to name a few, have graced the stage of the College's Science Center Theater.

In addition to the Lively Arts, the College's Fine Arts galleries in Blue Bell and Pottstown host more than a dozen exhibits annually featuring the work of renowned local and regional artists, as well as student, faculty, and alumni artists.

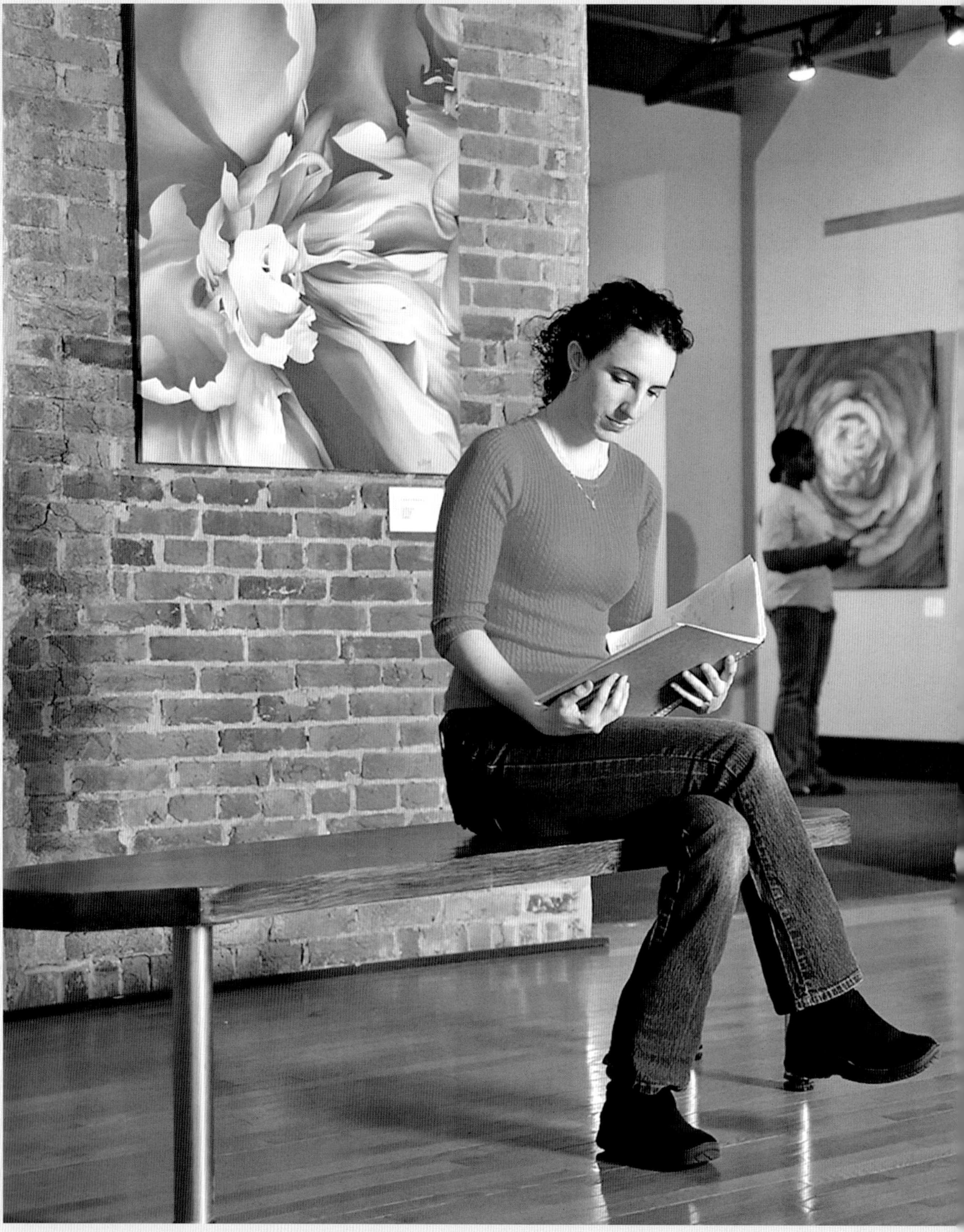

The West Campus Fine Arts Gallery provides students and the community with the opportunity to experience various forms of art.

Assistant Professor of Fine Arts Patrick Winston teaches drawing at the College's West Campus.

Theatre Arts students recycled defunct musical instruments to decorate a newspaper box on behalf of the Settlement Music School, Willow Grove, for Creative Montco's Artbox Competition on May 3, 2014.

Associate Professor of English Patricia Nestler chats with Norman Mailer at the College's Writers Conference in 2005.

Jazz vocalist Abbey Lincoln performs in the Science Center Theater on February 25, 2008.

College President Dr. Karen A. Stout talks with Hotel Rwanda hero Paul Ruseabagina during the 2007 Richard K. Bennett Distinguished Lectureship for Peace and Social Justice on February 26, 2007.

1993

- Community Day is held for the first time at the Central Campus.

1994

- The College hosts its first Technology & Learning Conference, designed for regional educators and IT professionals.

1995

- Distance learning options are offered for the first time.

- The College launches its first website. Faculty, staff, and students are assigned email addresses.

1996

- The West Campus in Pottstown opens at 101 College Drive.

- Campuses are renamed Central Campus in Blue Bell and West Campus in Pottstown.

THE COLLEGE EXPANDS INTO POTTSTOWN

THE VISION FOR A LEARNING SITE in Pottstown began long before Montgomery County Community College's West Campus opened its doors to approximately 300 students in the fall of 1996. In fact, as early as 1982, then-President Emeritus Dr. LeRoy Brendlinger was engaging Pottstown-area influencers in discussions about a potential second campus.

By the mid-1980s, the Board of Trustees opened offsite outreach centers in Pottstown and Upper Perkiomen to provide prospective students in western Montgomery County with College information, and in 1986, the Board formally appointed a Pottstown Center Advisory Committee.

A 1989 needs assessment survey cited three areas within the county that required the College's attention, including the western third part of the county—the area the Board ultimately determined was most in need of the College's services. Groundbreaking for what is now the South Hall building at the College's West Campus in Pottstown took place on May 12, 1995.

From its humble beginnings, the West Campus has thrived in Pottstown, growing its enrollment from just under 300 to more than 3,000 and expanding to four buildings—three of which are repurposed historic landmarks within the borough.

The former Vaughn Knitting Mill/Kiwi Shoe Polish Factory at 16 High Street is now North Hall, which houses classrooms, music and computer laboratories, and an art gallery.

The former PECO Power Station/EPA Brownfield site at 140 College Drive is now a three-acre Riverfront Academic and Heritage Center, which houses the offices of the Schuylkill River National and State Heritage Area, an outdoor amphitheater, and includes space for future classrooms.

And the former train station baggage claim building at 95 South Hanover Street is now the College's University Center, where select four-year colleges and universities offer bachelor and graduate degrees.

The College's original building, South Hall, located at 101 College Drive, houses classrooms, science and computer laboratories, the library, the Student Success Center, the Health Career Suite, and a cafeteria—amenities that make West a full-service campus for residents of the tri-county region.

74 | MONTGOMERY COUNTY COMMUNITY COLLEGE 50 YEARS OF THINKING BIG

The original building at the College's West Campus in Pottstown, South Hall.

Former Pottstown mayor Ann Jones leads College, borough, and county officials in the groundbreaking ceremony for the new Pottstown campus.

College officials sign a transfer agreement with Albright College in the late 1990s.

College officials accept a $250,000 federal grant to fund West Campus expansion on December 17, 2004.

Board Chairman James Mullen at the dedication ceremony for the West Campus in 1996.

1997

❧ The radio show *Montgomery County Community College On the Air* is broadcast for the first time.

2001

- Dr. Karen A. Stout becomes the fourth College president.

DR. KAREN A. STOUT NAMED FOURTH PRESIDENT

Dr. Karen A. Stout assumed the role as the fourth president of Montgomery County Community College in April 2001. Since that time, she has led the College with visionary thinking, strategic planning, and student success at the heart of her work. Under her leadership, the College has earned national recognition for its work in student access and success as an Achieving the Dream Leader College, and as a leader in sustainability, veterans services, technology, and academic innovation.

Dr. Stout's service and leadership extend well beyond the College to include numerous regional and national associations. She served as chair of the President's Advisory Board to the Community College Research Center at Columbia University Teacher's College, as a member of the American Association of Community Colleges Board of Directors, as a commissioner with the Middle States Commission on Higher Education, and as co-chair of the county's 21st Century Initiative Implementation Steering Committee.

Her well-respected advocacy efforts in Harrisburg and Washington, D.C. have progressed the community college mission nationally. In January 2014, on invitation from U.S. President Barack Obama, Dr. Stout participated in the White House College Opportunity Summit, committing to the implementation

Dr. Karen A. Stout with founding president Dr. LeRoy Brendlinger during a booksigning for Dr. Brendlinger's book From Swamp to Blue Bell *on March 22, 2005.*

Second Lady of the United States and community college professor Dr. Jill Biden talks with Dr. Karen A. Stout and student commencement speaker Antonio Marraro prior to the College's 2011 commencement ceremony, during which Dr. Biden provided the keynote address.

and growth of several College initiatives that help low-income and economically challenged students attain access to higher education. Also in 2014, she served as a panelist for the annual *U.S. News* STEM Solutions National Leadership Conference to discuss viable solutions for America's skills and education gap in the areas of science, technology, engineering, and math (STEM).

Among her many honors, Dr. Stout was named to the University of Delaware's Alumni Wall of Fame in 2005 for her outstanding professional and public service achievements. In 2006, she was named President of the Year by the American Student Association of Community Colleges (ASACC) and as Educator of the Year by the Tri-County Chamber of Commerce. She was also named as a Montgomery County Woman of Distinction in 2009.

In 2012, Dr. Stout was honored as a recipient of the University of Delaware Presidential Citation for Outstanding Achievement, and later that year, she earned the North East Region Chief Executive Officer Award from The Association of Community College Trustees.

Before joining Montgomery County Community College, Dr. Stout served as vice president for institutional advancement and enrollment services at Camden County College, and as the Rohrer Campus CEO in New Jersey. She holds a doctorate in Educational Leadership and a bachelor's degree in English from the University of Delaware and a master's degree in Business Administration from the University of Baltimore.

2002

- The College launches its first comprehensive Honors program.

- The Alumni Hall of Fame is established by the College's Foundation, into which individuals are inducted annually.

The first class of inductees into the College's Alumni Hall of Fame in October 2003: (seated, from left) George Marks and Dr. Celeste Schwartz; (standing) Tim Connolly, Peggy Kerr, Clark DeLeon, Oscar Vance, and Michael D'Aniello, with College President Dr. Karen A. Stout.

2003

- The Health Career Suite opens at the West Campus, and programs in radiography, surgical technology, and medical assisting are introduced.

- Montco Radio begins streaming 24/7 via the Internet.

Cutting the ribbon at the grand opening of the West Campus Health Career Suite on October 22, 2003: (from left) Mike Bitner, Board of Trustees chairman; Edward Zale, assistant director, Eastern Pennsylvania Region, Bureau of Employer and Career Services; Dr. Karen A. Stout, president; Charlton Brown, Radiography student; Dr. Dean Foster, West Campus dean; and Dr. Vicki Bastecki-Perez, dean of Health and Physical Education.

MONTCO RADIO:
STREAMING 24/7 ONLINE

STUDENT RADIO AT MONTGOMERY COUNTY COMMUNITY COLLEGE dates back to the late 1960s, when it began as a student club to DJ music at the College's original campus in Conshohocken. In the early 1970s, the station gained an audience when its music and content was broadcast into the College Hall cafeteria at the Central Campus in Blue Bell. In 2003, the station began broadcasting on the Internet, making its content available off-campus for the first time.

After changing its name from WRFM to Montco Radio, the station moved into the College's Advanced Technology Center in 2007. There, it occupied a variety of retrofitted spaces until 2013, when the College allocated a dedicated, state-of-the-art broadcast studio just off the atrium.

The introduction of Campus Radio Workshops I and II as part of the College's Digital Audio Production program, launched in 2007, helped students produce more professional on-air content. As a result, in 2009, *College Media Journal* (CMJ) named Montco Radio as one of the top five college Internet-only stations in the country.

Today, Montco Radio can be heard internationally on the Internet by visiting montcoradio.com.

The 1976 WRFM club President and Production Manager Chris Gabriel.

Station Manager Chelsea Epstein cuts the ceremonial ribbon outside of Montgomery County Community College's new Montco Radio studio on March 13, 2013. Also pictured are: (from left) Montco Radio officers Andrew McBride and Paige Murray, College President Dr. Karen A. Stout, Assistant Station Manager David Tatasiciore, and Montco Radio officer Dan Grundy.

2004

✧ The Brendlinger Library in Blue Bell is named and dedicated in honor of founding president Dr. LeRoy Brendlinger.

Dr. Karen Stout congratulates founding president Dr. LeRoy Brendlinger during a ceremony renaming the College's Central Campus library "The Brendlinger Library" on November 15, 2004.

2006

- In partnership with the Montgomery County Workforce Investment Board, the College begins offering an accelerated GED preparatory course at its West Campus.

- Human Services faculty develop and launch the innovative Partnership on Work Enrichment and Readiness (POWER) program for people in mental health recovery.

- Eight students participate in the College's first-ever Alternative Spring Break Experience. Since that time, growing numbers of students have traveled across the United States performing service work with organizations like Habitat for Humanity and The Samaritan Woman during the College's Spring Break week.

- The College launches its University Center framework. By partnering with select four-year colleges and universities, graduates and community members can earn bachelor's, master's, and doctoral degrees conveniently at the College's campuses in Blue Bell and Pottstown.

- At the West Campus, North Hall opens in the former Kiwi Shoe Polish factory.

North Hall

Montgomery County
Community College

The atrium of the Advanced Technology Center at the Central Campus in Blue Bell.

86 | MONTGOMERY COUNTY COMMUNITY COLLEGE 50 YEARS OF THINKING BIG

2007

- The Advanced Technology Center is completed, becoming the first new classroom building at the College's Central Campus since 1972 and supporting new academic programs in digital broadcasting, digital audio production, biotechnology, and electronic gaming and simulation design.

The College broke ground on the Advanced Technology Center on November 18, 2005. Pictured breaking ground on the future site are: (from left) Trustees Joe Palmer and Ed Mullin, Representative Kate Harper, Senator John Rafferty, President Dr. Karen A. Stout, Representative Mike Gerber, Commissioner Ruth Damsker, Trustee Chairman Mike Bitner, and Trustee Thaddeus Smith.

The College dedicated the Advanced Technology Center, the first new classroom building on the College's Central Campus since 1972, on October 16, 2007. Pictured just moments after cutting the ceremonial ribbon are: (from left) Commissioner James Matthews, Communications student John Riley, Biotechnology student Elizabeth Neuman, Commissioner Thomas Ellis, Commissioner Ruth Damsker, President Dr. Karen A. Stout, and Trustees Anthony DiSandro, Gertrude Mann, and Joseph Palmer.

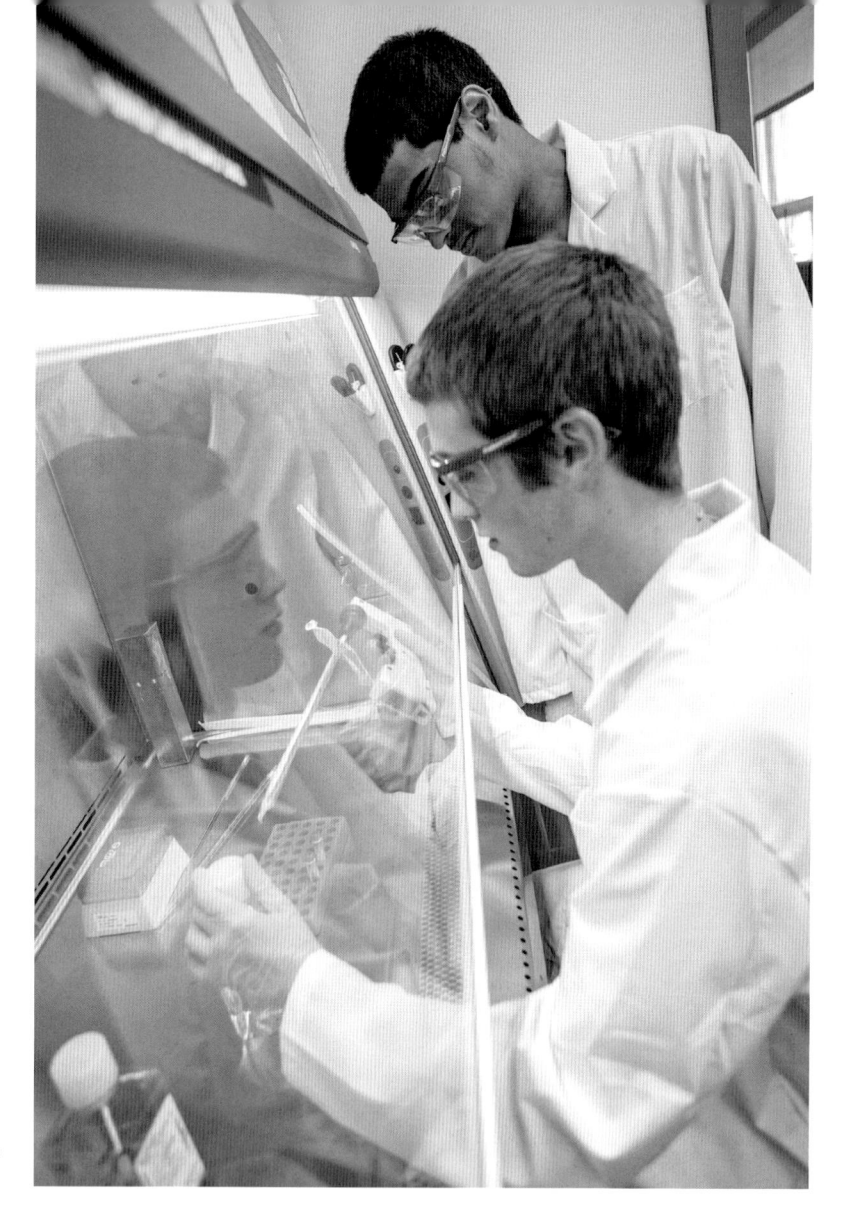

Right and below: State-of-the-art Biotechnology laboratories and digital audio/video production studios are housed in the Advanced Technology Center.

2007 (cont.)

- The College becomes one of only twenty-three IT Apple Authorized Training Centers in the country.

- The College is a charter signatory of the American College & University Presidents' Climate Commitment, pledging carbon neutrality by 2050.

CLIMATE LEADERSHIP

ENVIRONMENTAL SUSTAINABILITY ISN'T A NEW IDEA. In fact, the College's students and faculty have stressed the importance of a clean planet since the first Earth Day celebration in 1970. Fast forward forty-plus years and Montgomery County Community College isn't only advocating for environmental reform; it's leading the charge for climate responsibility in higher education.

In 2007, the institution became a charter signatory of the American College & University Presidents' Climate Commitment (ACUPCC), pledging carbon neutrality by 2050. Through its incorporation into strategic planning, core curriculum, and in everyday best practices as they relate to facilities management, campus operations, and transportation, sustainability has become a core value.

The College's sustainability efforts are led by a team of faculty, staff, students, alumni, and community residents who comprise the President's Climate Commitment Advisory Council. Chaired by College President Dr. Karen A. Stout, the Council developed the institution's first-ever Climate Commitment Action Plan, outlining short- and long-term strategies to reach carbon neutrality.

A system-wide approach to sustainability earned the College national attention when it received an Award for Institutional Excellence in Climate Leadership from Second Nature in 2011 and again in 2014—becoming the first community college to win twice. Institutions were evaluated based on a variety of criteria for climate leadership on campus, including senior leadership, learning experiences, innovative strategies and financing, student preparedness, climate innovation, and creation of opportunities.

Regionally, the College is consistently recognized by the Greater Valley Forge Transportation Management Association (GVF) for its work to reduce emissions through a variety of transportation strategies. The College earned GVF's 2011 Environmental Leadership Award as well as its Platinum Level Sustainability Award for three consecutive years.

The College holds annual celebrations on campus for Earth Day and Campus Sustainability Day.

The College introduced a transportation shuttle program that operated daily between the Central and West campuses in the fall of 2010. Combined with the ridesharing program Zimride, the two initiatives have reduced vehicle use by almost one million miles and carbon emissions by an estimated 54,644 metric tons to date.

Students wear gas masks to protest pollution at the College's original campus in Conshohocken in 1969.

Serena Dunlap, the 2013 president of the Student Environmental Sustainability Club, asks students to sign a sustainability pledge.

2007 (cont.)

- The College is named to the President's Higher Education Community Service Honor Roll by the Corporation for National and Community Service for the first time.

- A dedication ceremony is held for the pedestrian underpass at the West Campus, connecting North and South halls.

College and county officials dedicated the pedestrian underpass, which connected South Hall and North Hall for the first time on April 26, 2006, during a West Campus ten-year anniversary celebration.

2007 (cont.)

- The College enters into a partnership with Bucknell University's Community College Scholars Program through the Jack Kent Cooke Foundation.

- The College joins the national initiative "Achieving the Dream: Community Colleges Count," focusing on reducing the achievement gap for at-risk student populations.

ACHIEVING THE DREAM

WITH A COMPREHENSIVE APPROACH to student success, Montgomery County Community College is an Achieving the Dream Leader College that is recognized nationally for leveraging data to align budget decisions and strategic planning efforts with student success goals.

Since joining the Achieving the Dream initiative in 2006, the College has worked with national experts to identify strategies that improve student outcomes. Examples include improving persistence and success among students who place in pre-college level courses, reexamining targeted college-level courses—called gatekeeper courses—and reducing achievement gaps for specific cohorts of students.

The College has also implemented improved processes and programs to bolster students' first-year experience and transition to college based on systematic data analysis. Examples include improved new student orientation and registration processes, attendance reporting and mid-term grading requirements, reconfigured placement cut-off scores, a mandatory college orientation program for students placing in two or more developmental courses, and the Minority Student Mentoring Initiative.

The College has received several national accolades for its work in these areas. In 2011, the College received national recognition for its excellence in leveraging data to impact student success and completion during an annual Achieving the Dream Strategy Institute. Later that year, the College became one of seventy-one Achieving the Dream Leader Colleges in the country for its commitment to student success and sustained improvement on key student achievement indicators.

Then, in 2014, the College earned Achieving the Dream's prestigious Leah Meyer Austin Award, in recognition of its outstanding achievement in supporting and promoting student success through the creation of a culture of evidence, continuous improvement, systemic institutional change, broad engagement of stakeholders, and equity, with particular attention to low-income students and students of color.

Student Government Association leaders Christine Chiodo and Arthur Mongrande help spread the word about the College's Achieving the Dream Leader College designation in 2011.

2008

✣ The Mustangs Intercollegiate Athletics program is re-launched.

MUSTANGS ATHLETICS RETURNS TO CAMPUS

ATHLETICS WERE AN IMPORTANT PART OF STUDENT LIFE in the late 1960s, with Mustangs athletics teams competing in intercollegiate play as part of the Eastern Pennsylvania Community College Athletic Conference (EPCCAC). Early teams included men's soccer, basketball, golf, and wrestling, but the athletics program soon grew to include men's cross country and tennis and women's lacrosse, field hockey, basketball, and tennis.

Official intercollegiate play ended in 1989, although men's soccer and baseball teams continued to play extramural games against regional opponents into the 2000s. Then, in 2008—citing studies that show athletics programs can increase student enrollment and engagement among community colleges nationwide—the College re-introduced intercollegiate athletics.

After competing in a provisional season in 2008–2009, the Mustangs have since completed five successful seasons of intercollegiate play in Region 19 of the National Junior College Athletic Association (NJCAA) and the Eastern Pennsylvania Collegiate Conference (EPCC). Initial teams included men's and women's soccer and basketball, and men's baseball and women's softball, with women's volleyball added in 2010. The volleyball team won the regional championship in 2011, in only its second year of competition. In 2012, the College earned NJCAA's Region 19 Champion of Character Award, given annually to an institution that demonstrates outstanding results in character development in its student-athletes and coaches.

Mustangs women's soccer.

Mustangs women's basketball.

Above: Mustangs women's softball.

Right: Mustangs men's basketball.

Mustangs men's baseball.

2008 (cont.)

- The College is named one of the top technologically advanced community colleges in the country by the Center for Digital Education for the first time, going on to earn the designation for three consecutive years.

2009

- The Fine Arts Center renovation of the existing Art Barn is completed, and the College introduces a new Associate in Fine Arts (A.F.A.) degree program.

The College broke ground on the renovation and expansion of the Art Barn on April 11, 2007.

The completed Fine Arts Center opened in the spring of 2009.

2009 (cont.)

- The College is named a "Military Friendly School" by Victory Media for the first time.

VETERANS FIND SUPPORT, COMPASSION, AND CAMARADERIE AT THE COLLEGE

VETERANS AFFAIRS HAS BEEN A PART of Montgomery County Community College since it opened in Conshohocken. The College's early days saw droves of veteran students enrolling in classes after returning from combat in Vietnam. The College recognized that these students required specialized advising as they sought to understand their education benefits and transition into a school and community setting from a combat environment.

As the number of veteran students decreased around the mid-1980s to early 1990s, the College's Veterans Affairs services were integrated into the Office of Student Activities. However, the influx of U.S. troops into the Middle East over the last two decades has once again brought the need for increased veterans services to the forefront, especially in light of what doctors now know about post-traumatic stress disorder.

With student veteran enrollment growing by 55 percent in the mid-2000s, the College reestablished a Veterans Affairs Office as part of its Student Success Center, complete with a dedicated veterans academic advisor. Over the next five years, those services expanded and the College was lauded as a "Military Friendly School" annually since 2009, positioning it among the top 20 percent of colleges and universities in the country for its veteran support services.

Today, a wide array of veterans' resources—orientation, advising, study groups, a lounge, and even yoga—makes the College eligible for "Military Friendly" status. However, it's the genuine compassion and commitment of the College's faculty and

Student military veterans join state, county, and College officials as they dedicate the Veterans Resource Center in November 2011.

Honor Guard at the College's 2013 Veterans Day observance ceremony.

staff behind these resources that is the true champion.

A unique group of faculty and staff—the Veterans Support Team—has taken on the charge of assisting student veterans in their transition from active duty to civilian life. Self-formed in 2007 out of a shared commitment to student veterans, the team includes representatives from advising, counseling, financial aid, enrollment services, academic affairs, business and finance, and veterans services.

Student veterans network in the Veterans Resource Center.

Veterans Team member and Associate Professor of Psychology Dr. Ann Marie Donohue explains: "Our goal is to make sure the infrastructure is aligned to support the success of our student veterans. We're able to respond to issues quickly because we're communicating and problem-solving across departments."

The Veterans Resource Center, a small farmhouse at the College's Central Campus, was renovated in 2012 with grant funding from the Collegiate Consortium for Workforce and Economic Development. The Center serves as a "home base" for student veterans and includes a lounge, meeting areas, and offices for Veterans Services staff. The VRC is also the hub for members of the College's Student Veterans Organization—an official chapter of the Student Veterans of America.

In 2014, the College was accepted into the U.S. Department of Veterans Affairs' Yellow Ribbon Program, which assists veterans who have returned or relocated to Pennsylvania after their service with out-of-state tuition costs covered by the Post-9/11 G.I. Bill.

Members of the College's Student Veterans Organization hosted the first annual Community Appreciation Dinner in 2013. Each year, the students host the dinner for military and civilian supporters from the College and community to recognize their contribution to student veterans.

Nursing program students raised funds in 2013 to purchase ten trees for the Trees for Troops national movement, in addition to $2,000 for the Wounded Warriors Walk. Pictured here, Senator Rafferty helps load the truck at Bustard's Christmas Trees in Lansdale on December 7, 2013, along with Justin Machain, coordinator of Veterans Services; Joe Long, student veteran and Engineering major; Lindsey Brady, Nursing student and Student Nurses Club co-president; Connie Fiorentino, Nursing instructor and Student Nurses Club co-advisor; and Christine Dunigan, assistant professor of Nursing and Student Nurses Club co-advisor.

2009 (cont.)

- The second floor of North Hall is completed at the West Campus.

2010

- A full-scale renovation to Parkhouse Hall is completed at the Central Campus.

President Dr. Karen A. Stout explains the scope of the renovations to Student Government President Patricia O'Malley following a groundbreaking ceremony on September 9, 2009.

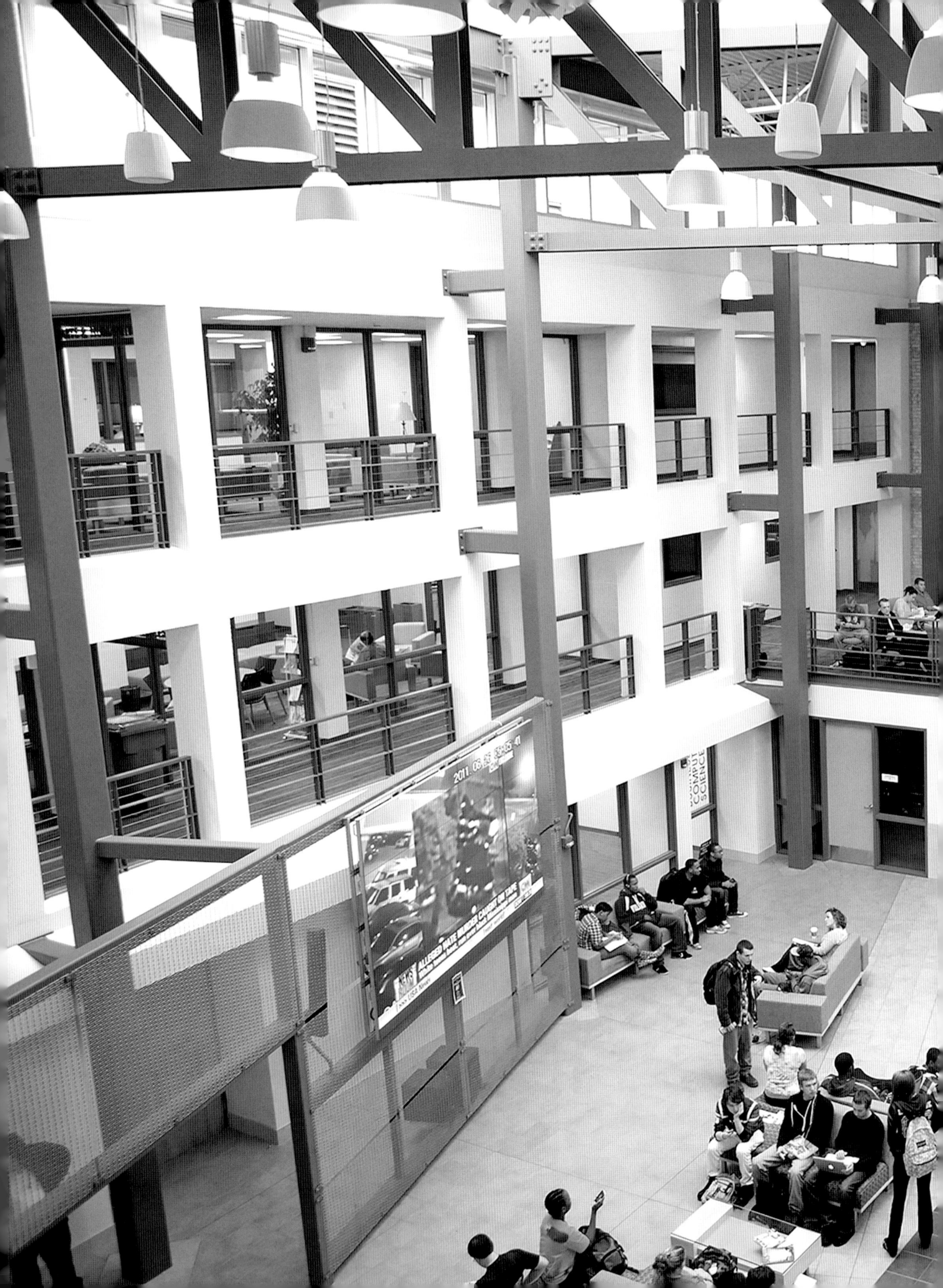
ALLEGED HATE MURDER CAUGHT ON TAPE
SCIENCE

The renovations filled in the existing courtyard to provide more useable space and gathering places for students without increasing the building's footprint.

2010 (cont.)

✣ The College receives a federal grant to establish an Upward Bound Program for at-risk high school youth in Norristown and Pottstown.

✣ The College begins work on the Riverfront Academic and Heritage Center in partnership with the Schuylkill River Heritage Area on the site of the former PECO building in Pottstown. Phase I, remediation of the parking lot, is completed.

College President Dr. Karen A. Stout and Director of Operations and Capital Projects Michael Billetta (center) cut the green ribbon during the parking lot dedication. Also pictured are: (from left) Pottstown Borough Council President Stephen Toroney, Pennsylvania Senator John C. Rafferty, Jr., Commissioner James Matthews, Director of the U.S. EPA's Middle-Atlantic Region Hazardous Site Cleanup Division, Kathryn Hodgkiss, Trustee Chairman Mike Bitner, U.S. Representative James Gerlach, Pennsylvania State Representative Thomas Quigley, and Commissioner Bruce Castor.

2010 (cont.)

- The redesigned developmental mathematics course Concepts of Numbers reaches full-scale implementation at the College. Developed by Assistant Professor of Mathematics Barbara Lontz, the curriculum changes the way in which developmental math is taught across the country.

- The National Association for the Education of Young Children awards the College's Children's Center exemplary status for Engaging Diverse Families.

- The College opens its Center for Entrepreneurial Studies and Business Incubator in Parkhouse Hall at the Central Campus.

- A new Children's Center opens at the Central Campus as a stand-alone building, doubling the Center's capacity from forty-two to eighty-four students.

Some of the College's youngest students—those from the Children's Center—helped College officials dedicate the new facility on February 22, 2010.

RIGHT: *Thousands of people attend the College's student-run International Festival each spring.*

BELOW: *College signage along High Street at the West Campus in Pottstown.*

108 | MONTGOMERY COUNTY COMMUNITY COLLEGE 50 YEARS OF THINKING BIG

ABOVE: *More than 3,500 cadets have graduated from the College's Municipal Police Academy.*

LEFT: *Board of Trustees Chairman Michael J. D'Aniello speaks about the importance of community college funding at the Pennsylvania Capitol in Harrisburg during the annual Community College Lobby Day.*

MONTGOMERY COUNTY COMMUNITY COLLEGE 50 YEARS OF THINKING BIG | 109

110 | MONTGOMERY COUNTY COMMUNITY COLLEGE 50 YEARS OF THINKING BIG

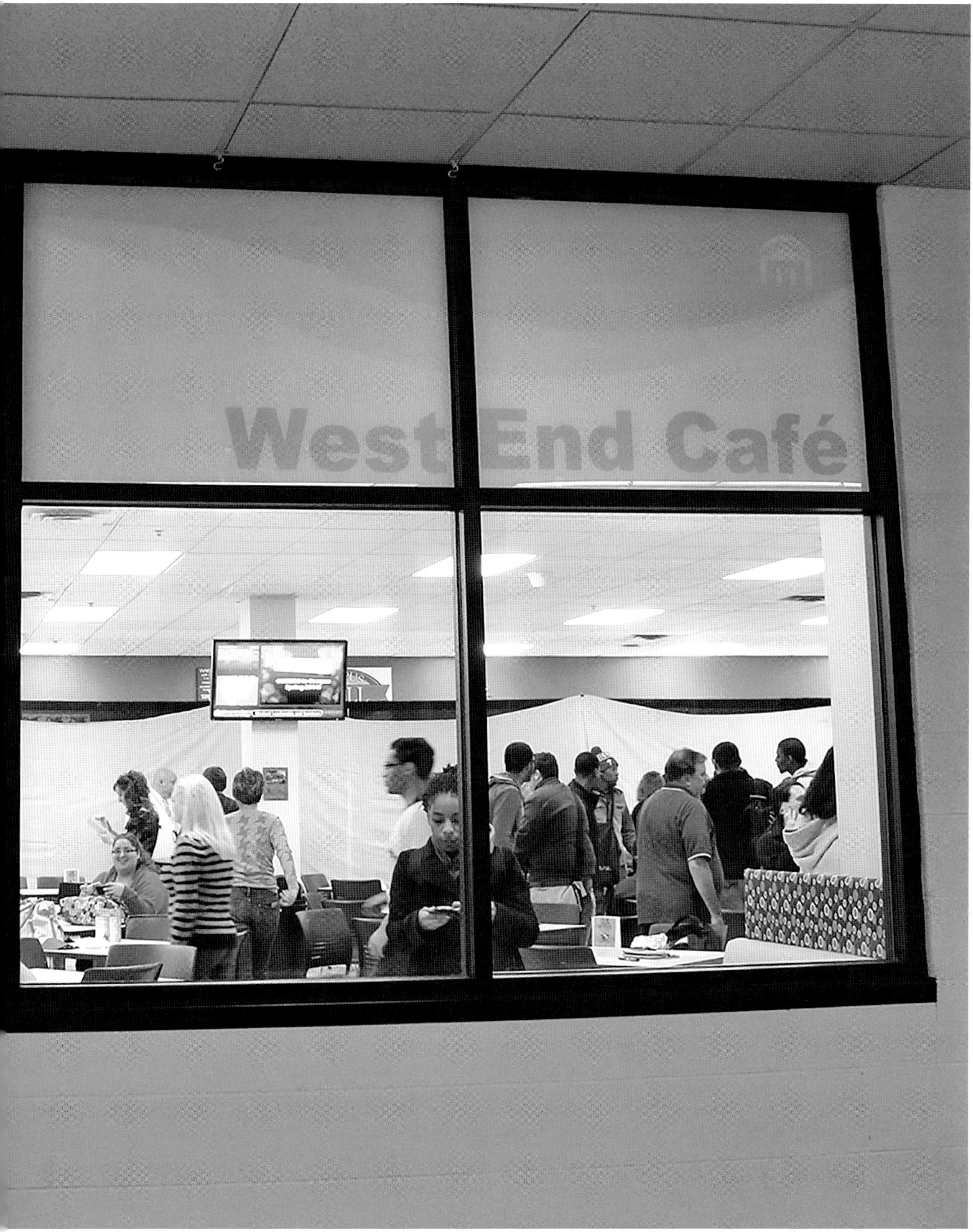
West End Café

2010 (cont.)

- A campus transportation shuttle begins operating between Blue Bell and Pottstown.

- The Black Box Theater and music suites open in the Science Center at the Central Campus.

Assistant Professor and Theatre Arts Coordinator Michael Whistler works with students in the Black Box Theater at the Central Campus.

2011

- The College is awarded Achieving the Dream Leader College status for its work to improve student learning outcomes.

- The College receives its first national Climate Leadership Award from Second Nature.

- The College joins the national "College Completion Challenge" and pledges to increase graduation rates by 50 percent by 2020.

The College held a Completion Pledge Rally on January 18, 2011. Pictured are: (from left) College President Dr. Karen A. Stout, Phi Theta Kappa President Chris Jensen, West Campus Student Government Association President Grace Pusey, Central Campus Student Government Association President Antonio Marrero, and Trustee Chairman Michael J. D'Aniello.

2011 (cont.)

- The College is selected to participate in the American Association of Community Colleges' Voluntary Framework of Accountability (VFA) pilot.

David Whalen teaches biology at the College's West Campus in Pottstown.

Above: A student browses the stacks in the West Campus Library.

Right: The West Campus Jazz Ensemble performs in the College's art gallery.

Below: Students host an annual West Campus Lasagna Dinner to raise money for community charities and student scholarships.

2012

- The Veterans Resource Center opens in the former "202 House" at the Central Campus.

- Phase II in the development of the Riverfront Academic and Heritage Center is completed at the West Campus.

Cutting the ribbon on Phase II of the Riverfront Academic and Heritage Center on February 6, 2012, are: (from left) Foundation Board Member Jack Koury, Trustee Chairman Michael D'Aniello, College President Dr. Karen A. Stout, and Pennsylvania Senator John Rafferty.

- The full-scale renovation to College Hall is completed at the Central Campus.

ABOVE: College Hall's exterior and interior got a full facelift.

LEFT: College Hall was re-dedicated on October 4, 2012, following full-scale renovation. Pictured are: (from left) Trustee Chairman Michael J. D'Aniello; Central Campus Student Government Association President Abu Chowdhury; Commissioners Leslie Richards, Josh Shapiro, and Bruce Castor; Senator John Rafferty; Trustee Geoffrey Brandon; College President Dr. Karen A. Stout; Trustee Susan Arnold; former trustee chairman Mike Bitner; and Executive Director of Enrollment Services Cindy Haney.

2012 (cont.)

- The University Center opens at the West Campus in the former the East Penn AAA building at 95 S. Hanover Street in Pottstown.

The University Center at the College's West Campus in Pottstown.

The College's West Campus in Pottstown is now comprised of four buildings. The University Center is in the background.

118 | MONTGOMERY COUNTY COMMUNITY COLLEGE 50 YEARS OF THINKING BIG

The Schuylkill River Academic and Heritage Center is in phase three of its development. It houses the offices of the Schuylkill River Heritage Center.

A unique feature of the Schuylkill River Academic and Heritage Center at the West Campus is its green roof.

2012 (cont.)

- The College receives NJCAA's Region 19 Champion of Character Award for demonstrating outstanding results in character development in its student-athletes and coaches.

2013

- The College enters its first international transfer agreement with Dongseo University in South Korea.

Montgomery County Community College announced its agreement with Dongseo University during a networking meeting of the Norristown Business Association at the law office of Joshua Chung on September 26, 2013. Helping to facilitate the agreement are: (from left) John Pak, Jordan Winquist, and John Chung, along with College President Dr. Karen A. Stout, Vice President of Student Affairs and Enrollment Management Dr. Kathrine Swanson, and Trustee Moon Ahn.

- The Virtual Campus is introduced, laying the groundwork for an innovative approach to online learning.

VIRTUAL CAMPUS

IN HIS 1993 CONVOCATION SPEECH to the College community, Dr. Edward Sweitzer addressed the need for a distance learning division within the College. The program was up and running by 1995; students engaged in course curriculum outside of the classroom via print materials, video, audiocassettes, television, teleconferencing, and a few years later, hybrid and fully online courses. By 1998, close to 1,200 students had engaged in some form of distance learning.

Today, students can complete a number of degrees and certificates fully online from anywhere in the world through the College's Virtual Campus. Introduced in 2013, the Virtual Campus adds wrap-around services—advising, career services, disability services, and tutoring—to the online classroom, giving virtual students access to the same critical services as those students in a traditional classroom setting.

2013 (cont.)

- The College is selected to participate in Gateway to College, a program that partners the College with area school districts to help students at risk of not completing high school to graduate and go to college.

- The Mustangs mascot is introduced.

The College's Mustangs mascot has become a favorite on campus and in the community.

2013 (cont.)

- The Culinary Arts Institute opens in Towamencin Town Square, Lansdale, in support of the expanded Culinary Arts and Pastry Arts curriculum.

THE CULINARY ARTS INSTITUTE AT MONTGOMERY COUNTY COMMUNITY COLLEGE

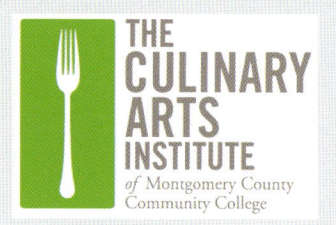

IN RESPONSE TO GROWING employment opportunities in the food and hospitality industries, Montgomery County Community College introduced a Chef Apprenticeship degree program in the fall of 2003. A few years later, the program evolved from an apprenticeship model into a more comprehensive A.A.S. degree program with Culinary Arts and Pastry Arts options.

Despite its popularity, the program remained small; lack of an on-site teaching kitchen meant classes could only be held in the evening through a partnership with a local vocational high school. Knowing the program had far more potential, the College began looking for a more permanent home.

Coincidentally, the Philadelphia Suburban Development Corporation (PSDC) had recently begun work on a major project—the Towamencin Town Square complex—just seven miles away from the College's Central Campus. With plans for a hotel, apartments, restaurants, offices, and more, the complex seemed like a perfect fit for a state-of-the-art culinary school. The College and PSDC agreed to a ten-year lease, with options for an extension, and a groundbreaking ceremony took place on March 23, 2012.

In August 2013, the brand-new Culinary Arts Institute opened its doors to approximately 120 students—with projected enrollment reaching 350 students over the next five years. The 15,000-square-foot facility features four teaching kitchens, three smart classrooms, a retail shop for coffee and baked goods, and a first-floor patio for dining and grilling. In addition to A.A.S. degrees in Culinary and Pastry Arts, the Institute offers a one-year certificate and a full array of Culinary Enthusiast courses for the community.

The College celebrated the opening of its new Culinary Arts Institute on August 23, 2013, with a ribbon-cutting. Pictured are: (from left) Representative Kate Harper, Commissioner Leslie Richards, Trustee Chairman Michael D'Aniello, CAI Director and Chef Francine Marz, College President Dr. Karen A. Stout, Philadelphia Suburban Development Corporation Vice President Mark Nicoletti, former student Tom Sergio, and Dean of Business and Entrepreneurial Initiatives Phil Needles.

MONTGOMERY COUNTY COMMUNITY COLLEGE 50 YEARS OF THINKING BIG | 123

2013–14 Student Government Association Presidents Jeremiah Garcia and Maggie Kanter put letters in a time capsule during the kickoff of the College's fiftieth anniversary celebration.

The College's students, faculty, staff, and alumni engaged in "50 Acts of Kindness" as part of the 50th Anniversary celebration. Pictured left, Culinary Arts students baked a colonial birthday cake and other refreshments to help celebrate George Washington's birthday at the Valley Forge National Historical Park. At right, more than 100 members of the College's Administrative Staff spent a day of service volunteering at five sites throughout Montgomery County in June.

As part of the College's 50th Anniversary celebration, Dr. Lee Bender, Professor of Economics, and Dr. Celeste Schwartz, Vice President for Technology and College Services, provided the 2014 Commencement keynote address. Both have worked at the College for more than forty years, and Celeste is also an alumna.

2014

- President Dr. Karen A. Stout is invited by U.S. President Barack Obama to attend the White House College Opportunity Summit on January 16, 2014, to share the College's initiatives to help low-income and economically challenged students attain access to higher education.

- The College receives the Leah Meyer Austin Award from Achieving the Dream for its continued efforts to improve student access and success.

- The College receives its second Climate Leadership Award from Second Nature, becoming the first community college to earn multiple awards from the organization.

- President Dr. Karen A. Stout serves as a panelist for the annual *U.S. News* STEM Solutions National Leadership Conference to discuss viable solutions for America's skills and education gap in the areas of science, technology, engineering, and math (STEM).

- Wind turbines (West Campus) and solar panels (Central Campus) are installed as part of the College's Guaranteed Energy Savings Agreement with Siemens Industries, Inc.

- Two alumni, Joseph Sapienza and Sean King, direct *The History of Montco: A Documentary*. The three-hour film will be available in the College's libraries.

- Plans are finalized for the Physical Education Center to undergo renovations to become a comprehensive Health Science Center at the Central Campus.

Architect rendering of the future Health Science Center.

Twenty-five-foot vertical axis wind turbines were recently installed outside of the College's Schuylkill Riverfront Academic and Heritage Center at 140 College Drive, adjacent to Riverfront Park and the Schuylkill River. While the turbines won't power major facilities on campus, the demo project will provide real-life teaching and learning opportunities for West Campus students and faculty. The turbines were dedicated on April 21, 2014.

Joseph Sapienza and Sean King